Music,
     Metaphor,
               Imagery,
Meaning . . .

These are but a few of the tools of the poet—techniques which must be comprehended if the reader is to experience the illumination and pleasure that poetry can offer.

Using examples that range from Homer to Shakespeare to Pope to Keats to Browning to Robert Lowell and Lawrence Ferlinghetti, Burton Raffel scrutinizes the ways in which poets of every age have created poems that have moved and involved and often changed the hearts and minds of men. And Mr. Raffel cites poetic failures as well as triumphs, to give the student of poetry a foundation for individual critical judgment.

Dealing with remarkable clarity, in areas too often clouded by hazy thinking and fuzzy rhetoric, and clearly demonstrating his own personal involvement and love of the art, Burton Raffel has written an introduction to poetry that is at once lively, thought-provoking, engrossing, and essential.

POEMS: AN ANTHOLOGY, edited by Burton Raffel, is designed as a companion volume to IN-TRODUCTION TO POETRY.

The SIGNET CLASSIC Poetry Series

☐ **THE SELECTED POETRY OF BROWNING.** Edited by George Ridenour   (#CQ313—95¢)

☐ **THE SELECTED POETRY OF BYRON.** Edited by W. H. Auden   (#CQ346—95¢)

☐ **THE SELECTED POETRY OF DONNE.** Edited by Marius Bewley   (#CQ343—95¢)

☐ **THE SELECTED POETRY OF DRYDEN.** Edited by John Arthos   (#CW496—$1.50)

☐ **THE SELECTED POETRY OF GEORGE HERBERT.** Edited by Joseph H. Summers (#CY366—$1.25)

☐ **THE SELECTED POETRY OF KEATS.** Edited by Paul de Man   (#CQ325—95¢)

☐ **THE SELECTED POETRY OF MARVELL.** Edited by Frank Kermode   (#CQ363—95¢)

☐ **THE COMPLETE POETRY AND SELECTED CRITICISM OF EDGAR ALLAN POE.** Edited by Allen Tate   (#CY384—$1.25)

☐ **THE SELECTED POETRY OF POPE.** Edited by Martin Price   (#CY495—$1.25)

☐ **THE SELECTED POETRY AND PROSE OF SIDNEY.** Edited by David Kalstone   (#CY498—$1.25)

☐ **THE SELECTED POETRY OF SHELLEY.** Edited by Harold Bloom   (#CQ342—95¢)

☐ **THE SELECTED POETRY OF SPENSER.** Edited by A. C. Hamilton   (#CY350—$1.25)

☐ **THE SELECTED POETRY AND PROSE OF WORDSWORTH.** Edited by G. H. Hartman   (#CY506—$1.25)

INTRODUCTION TO POETRY

by Burton Raffel

A MENTOR BOOK from
NEW AMERICAN LIBRARY
TIMES MIRROR
New York and Toronto
The New English Library Limited, London

MENTOR TRADEMARK REG. U.S. PAT. OFF. AND FOREIGN COUNTRIES
REGISTERED TRADEMARK—MARCA REGISTRADA
HECHO EN CHICAGO, U.S.A.

SIGNET, SIGNET CLASSICS, SIGNETTE, MENTOR AND PLUME BOOKS
are published *in the United States* by
The New American Library, Inc.,
1301 Avenue of the Americas, New York, New York 10019,
in Canada by The New American Library of Canada Limited,
295 King Street East, Toronto 2, Ontario,
in the United Kingdom by The New English Library Limited,
Barnard's Inn, Holborn, London, E.C. 1, England.

FIRST PRINTING, APRIL, 1971

PRINTED IN THE UNITED STATES OF AMERICA

for Mia—
with whom and for whom
I became a poet

There will never be a first-rate poet or a first-rate critic who lacks a first-rate ear; and no one will ever acquire a first-rate ear without working for it. . . . Poetry, alas, like painting and music, is an art—it is not a form of happy self-indulgence; and to master an art or even understand it, one has to labor with all of one's mind and with at least a part of one's body.
—Yvor Winters, *The Function of Criticism*

Scribendi recte sapere est et principium et fons. Good sense is everything, in art.
—Horace, *The Art of Poetry*

Preface

This book has been written for the beginning student of poetry. It can be used, I think, by a student working on his own; it will be better used by students enrolled in poetry classes, at whatever level.

I have tried to explain everything which might give a beginner trouble—technical terms, difficult allusions, obscure or obsolete words. The index is very full, and is cross-referenced. I have however not written down to the beginner: one chief assumption of this book is, as it always is in my own classes, that the teacher is neither more (nor less) than *primus inter pares*, first among equals. Or, as George Orwell put it, everybody is equal, but some people are more equal than others.

I had intended, at first, to provide the book with a glossary—a kind of small dictionary of working, technical terms. But as the book has gotten itself written, I have slowly realized that I do not generally approve of technical literary terms. And the ones I do approve of, which are of course the ones I myself use, have each and all been defined in the text, and those definitions can easily be found, and read in context, by using the Index.

Many poems are quoted from; not many are quoted in their entirety. (All quotations are identified, by both author and title, in the index.) In reproducing poetry I have fairly consistently modernized spelling, capitalization and, often, punctuation. I see no reason, for example, to reproduce the Elizabethan spelling of "chaines of peble stone" or "she ware no gloues," when I can substitute the more accessible, and in no important way different, "chains of pebble stone" and "she wore no gloves." I have—though very carefully, since here changes in spelling can produce changes in poetic music—slightly modernized even the selections from Chaucer, in chapter five.

CONTENTS

INTRODUCTION
TO
POETRY

CHAPTER ONE: What Poetry Means

People have been arguing for years about what Good means, what Bad means—and what Poetry means. Trying to define poetry, however, seems to me a bit like trying to define life itself. A really wise man would answer, if asked "What is life?", with "Don't define it. Live it." I have the same feeling about poetry. There are many definitions, but they seem to me to tell you more about what the definer wants you to know (and more, too, about the definer himself), than they tell you about poetry. I'm interested in the poem itself. And poems tell you a great deal, if you know how to listen. But you have to learn their language, just as you have to learn a Frenchman's or a Spaniard's, if you want to understand what they say.

> So shoots a star as doth my mistress glide
> At midnight through my chamber . . .

This is the opening of a poem by John Davies of Hereford, writing about 1605. It's not a terribly complex poem, or a difficult poem—but it does give off a whole host of signals, in just these two lines, signals which help us to read it as it was meant to be read. Davies lets us know, at once, that he is writing a love poem (not a treatise on astronomy, not a tract on political behavior). It is a heterosexual love poem, and the lover/poet writes approvingly of both love and the particular object of his affections. It is not a mocking poem, it is not a satire; there is no irony in these opening lines. This is important: if the poet were to only *seem* to be praising love and women and his particular woman, then we would have to listen to him differently, knowing that he was in fact saying something different from what he might at first seem to be saying. But there is no doubt here: John Davies not only likes love and women and his woman, but he feels confident that his woman likes him. If she did not, would she visit him "at midnight," in his bedroom? Would she come gliding, would she make so glowing an entrance ("so shoots a star")?

These are important matters: we already know a great deal about the poem, when we know this much, and we are thereby much better fitted to read it. But there is more to be learned, even from just these two lines. The other signals are perhaps less obvious, but they are no less real—and no less important. Approval of nature and its beauty is expressed. Indeed, the poet carefully links his appreciation and approval of his woman with his appreciation and approval of natural beauty. To his mind, clearly, such a link strengthens each side, nature and his woman both. He indicates, too, that the nature he admires is not static but alive, in motion: a shooting star. Now this is a very basic statement of values—and it is not something we can assume, though as it happens we in our time share John Davies' views. The great German poet, Goethe, did not.

A hundred and fifty years after John Davies wrote these lines, Goethe was making his first trip to Italy. Crossing the Alps, he kept the window shades on his carriage carefully down—except once, when he raised a shade, looked out (very doubtfully), and then cried "Mountains: ugh!" and promptly pulled the shade down again. Inevitably, this sort of attitude will affect a man's poetry. It affected Goethe's; the contrary attitude, as we have seen, affected John Davies'. Fifty years after Goethe's Italian trip, William Wordsworth passed through the Alps, and loved every rock, every flower, every cliff. Things had changed, and Wordsworth was already a very different kind of man, in this respect, than Goethe had been. I've not said that Wordsworth was better, or that he was worse, but only that he was different. And because he was different, his poetry was different too. Poets are neither more nor less human than other people, and poetry, which is simply what poets do, is a completely human activity. If indeed there is a single, primary assumption in this book, it is that poetry is an activity as natural as (but no more natural than) playing, singing, or working—no matter what one works at.

> Now's the time for mirth and play,
> Saturday's an holiday;
> Praise to heaven unceasing yield,
> I've found a lark's nest in the field.

Adult poets don't usually write real children's poetry; usually they write what they think a child should like, and at best they manage to cater to what they think the child's taste is. Christopher Smart, who wrote these lines about 1770, was what the textbooks call "intermittently mad." That is, he had an uncertain ability to function "normally": society's values—*his* society's values, in his time, and in his place—were rarely firm and uppermost in his mind. He paid a substantial price for this "instability": one of his most famous poems, "A Song to David," is traditionally said to have been scrawled on the walls of a madhouse, and Smart lived neither a long nor a fulfilled life. But he also achieved—or maintained—perceptions and sensitivities which adults don't ordinarily have. The association of "praise to heaven unceasing yield" and "I've found a lark's nest in the field," is not only one which most adults would not make, or be capable of making, but it is precisely the kind of association (or dissociation) which children and madmen do make. And we are learning, in our time, that the insights of children and madmen, which travel along the paths of a logic which is different from our usual logic, but are no less valid for all that, have a strangely high order of utility in the madhouse which, increasingly, we understand that our world is. (See the British psychiatrist R. D. Laing's books, and especially his *Politics and Experience,* which argues that "schizophrenic" politics are, in our time, the only sane politics, and "sane" politics are in fact uselessly schizophrenic.)

What Christopher Smart is doing, then, is asserting both the facts of the child's state of mind *and* the child's right to be what he is. At one time children were conceived of as merely adults-in-training, even miniature adults: consider the early Renaissance paintings in which children are simply tiny adults—small, yes, but built to an adult scale and then reduced in size. The full emotional quality of Smart's lines, I think, is therefore much more significant than a quick reading reveals. Not that Smart was consciously "revolutionary," or anxious to replace his society's values with the related but different values he had formed. Rather, Smart was a man as well as a poet; he could not help being what he was, and writing his poetry out of that being, with all its differences and changes in emphasis. Again, the important thing is to approach the poetry with the assumption that it represents a man talking to other men, not some mystical, magical production unrelated to normal human activities. ("Oh *him!* He's a poet." Or: "That's just *poetry.*")

Five years have past; five summers, with the length
Of five long winters! and again I hear
These waters, rolling from their mountain-springs
With a soft inland murmur. —Once again
Do I behold these steep and lofty cliffs,
That on a wild secluded scene impress
Thoughts of more deep seclusion . . .

Wordsworth is not as simple a poet, not even in his language, as he sometimes liked to think, but there is nothing *visibly* complex about "Five years have past; five summers, with the length/ Of five long winters!" I have always felt a deep, even a passionate sense of mystery in these words. (This is the opening of one of Wordsworth's greatest poems, dully titled "Lines composed a few miles above Tintern Abbey, on revisiting the banks of the Wye during a tour, July 13, 1798.") The mystery is in the language, of course: everything in poetry is in the language, since poetry is as much language as painting is paint or sculpture is stone. But the mystery is also something more than words, something which underlies the words, something which comes from Wordsworth the man and finds expression, here, in his poetry. Wordsworth's sense of the measured passage of time, and his empathy with nature, are extraordinary. He seems to feel, in time's mere movement, a wonder that transcends his own personal odyssey, his own progress toward experience and understanding. "Five . . . five . . . five . . .": he tolls the numbers like immensely reflective bells. It is in fact a sacerdotal moment for him, a kind of worship of the most-holy. It is Time, and it is rolling waters, and it is mountains (all of them large, grand, primal characteristics), and from each and all of them there is a feedback, a swelling sense of "thoughts of more deep seclusion . . . ." Wordsworth *feels* his steps, on this walking tour, as he feels the hours as he feels the water as he feels the mountains. His journey down the banks of the River Wye, his re-*vision* of scenes once precious to him, is a passionately mysterious moment because he carries within himself all the moments past, and in a way also the inchoate sense of moments to come. (It's something of a nineteenth-century characteristic: Walt Whitman used to try to peer up out of the page, into the future, and talk to his unborn readers. "I am with you, you men and women of a generation, or ever so many generations hence./ Just as you feel when you look on the river and sky, so I felt . . .") Wordsworth is not himself sure just what is pushing at him. He knows that the world he sees is overcast with a coloring of emotions and thoughts, no matter how imperfectly comprehended, and that he and this world of his are somehow moving together. (As he puts it in another poem, "Rolled round in earth's diurnal course/ With rocks, and stones, and trees.")

But what does this add up to, for Wordsworth or for us? This poetry is less precise than the Elizabethan or the eighteenth-century poetry I have already quoted. Not all Romantic poetry is imprecise, but much of it is. And there are reasons for the imprecision. The Romantics began the conscious discovery of the internal world, the world of the human psyche—and this is not a world with clear outlines and reliable maps. Wordsworth is definitely in strong, vivid relation to the world we see with our eyes, but if he is a "nature" poet it is nature poetry with a difference. Chaucer begins his *Canterbury Tales* with a nature description— "Whan that Aprill with his showers soote/ The droghte of March hath perced to the roote" (soote-sweet, droghte-drought)—and he is not simply painting a scene. Nature for Chaucer is an affective reality, he *feels* just as much as he *sees*. But he is reacting to generally understood natural phenomena: after the long cold winter, and the barren dryness of March, the spring rains are sweet—not just to Chaucer, and not just in a particular year, but to many many people in many many times (and climes). But Chaucer is *not* examining himself in a natural mirror, he is not in any sense fusing (and certainly is not confusing) himself with nature. Wordsworth, who is often loosely called a "pantheist" (someone who identifies nature with God, and God with nature), finds *himself* in nature. He often talks about nature as a teacher, even the greatest of teachers: "One impulse from a vernal wood/ May teach you more *of man,/ Of moral evil and of good,/* Than all the sages can." (Italics added) Nature for him is not simply a person, or a personage, but a transcendent reality in which man too has a role, and in which he can see, can discover, his own nature—and the pun is deliberate.

For Wordsworth, then, and pretty much for all the Romantics and for many of those who come after them, nature, and experience generally, do not exist as separate phenomena, objective, independent of man. They exist because they are perceived; they are meaningful because man can see his own meaning in them, can trace some of the patterns of his own inner being. Matthew Arnold put it bluntly (and lamely) in his "Dover Beach." Talking of the sound of ocean waves, he first claims that when

Sophocles "heard it on the Aegean . . . it brought/ Into his mind the turbid ebb and flow/ Of human misery." Then he adds: "we/ Find also in the sound a thought." The poetry isn't very good, but the thought is very plain—and it is also the very obvious descendant of Wordsworth. By the 1960's Wordsworth's influence had been so often absorbed, and digested, and redigested, and the world of men (and therefore of poetry) had changed so much, that Alan Dugan could begin a poem about childhood, "Thesis, Antithesis, and Nostalgia," like this:

> Not even dried-up leaves,
> skidding like ice-boats on
> their points down winter streets,
> can scratch the surface of
> a child's summer and its wealth . . .

Dugan is still, no matter how differently, using nature perceptions to explore psychological ones. Wordsworth would more likely have said that *he* explored *moral* perceptions, but it's not accidental that he succeeded in writing only two of the three parts of the great moral poem he was determined to write, and that only the first part, which is a detailed examination of his own psychology, its growth and its changes, is really good poetry—is often great poetry. (That first part of the overall moral poem is usually known as *The Prelude;* my own edition of the first part uses Wordsworth's own working title, namely *The Poem to Coleridge.*) And Alan Dugan's dry leaves, skating down frozen streets, are in the end not very different from Wordsworth and his boyhood friends, "[hissing] along the polished ice . . . while far distant hills/ Into the tumult sent an alien sound/ Of melancholy not unnoticed . . ."

It is important to realize, it seems to me, that poetry's boundaries are man's boundaries, neither more nor less. Anthropological home truths are relatively widely accepted, these days: a black man is not implicitly inferior to a white man, but only blacker than a white man; a native of Ottawa will of course feel and think rather differently from a native of St. Louis—and a native of Mexico City will inevitably think and feel very differently from either of them. Not many people would seriously argue, today, that a dirty Spaniard is less "civilized" than a clean Texan, or that anything but cultural conditioning is responsible for the ways in which the French and the Germans think and feel and act differently. These same kinds of differences, though they will be expressed differently, are necessarily going to occur in the poetry written by these differing peoples. (This is one of the principal fascinations for the translator of poetry.) Shakespeare is in my own view probably the greatest poet of any language and any period, but he is definitely not a standard by which poets of other languages and cultures can always be shaped—or evaluated. (Samuel Johnson said, neatly, that "The merit of Shakespeare was such as the ignorant could take in, and the learned add nothing to.") Different peoples, different times, require different things of poets, just as they do of engineers, architects, chemists, and generals.

> With a lantern,
> Someone walking in the night,
> Through the plum trees.

This is a *haiku* (translated by a wild and wonderful eccentric, R. H. Blyth). It would be hard to think of this poem as anything but Japanese: the stamp of Japanese culture is all over it, from the delicate light image to the dark plum trees. (I wonder if any Japanese writer has ever done a comparative study of Wordsworth's view of nature and the nature so lovingly, and so differently, portrayed by his own country's poets?) But it is important to realize that all cultures are human, and therefore inevitably overlapping to at least some extent: if the Japanese *haiku*-poet is superemphatically oriental, what is the Indonesian poet, Chairil Anwar?

> The last time you came
> You brought flowers,
>
> Red roses, white jasmine,
> Blood and holiness,
> And spread them in front of me
> With a wondering look: for you.
>
> We were stunned
> And asked each other: what's this?
> Love? Neither of us understood.
>
> That day we were together.
> We did not touch.
>
> But oh my heart that will not give itself
> Break, you bastard, ripped by your loneliness!

(The translation is my own.) Any Western poet would be proud to have written this. Not many have been good enough.

Poetry does not live by culture alone: I don't want to be misunderstood. The kind of *meaning* I have been talking about, so far, is historically and culturally conditioned, but it is not reducible to any easy, simplistic formula. And the complexities involved are even more complicated than simply variables of history and culture: this too is extremely important to understand. A poet can say one thing one day, another thing the next day—which does not mean that he is, somehow, inherently unreliable, unstable, fickle, even weak-minded. (There are lots of people who honestly believe that poetry is a kind of disease of the mind. But there are also increasingly large numbers who believe that buying and selling stocks and bonds, or designing plastic grass, is a disease of the soul.) People change in just this way, day by day, even hour by hour. A lucky accident, an unexpected smile, a delightful kiss, can lift the man (and the poet he happens also to be) just as quickly as an unlucky accident, an unexpected scowl, and a swift kick, can drop him down, depressed and miserable.

> Much have I travelled in the realms of gold,
> And many goodly states and kingdoms   [goodly-large]
>   seen;
> Round many western islands have I been
> Which bards in fealty to Apollo hold.
>   [bards-poets; Apollo-god of poetry]

John Keats wrote this, in 1815, after an orgy of reading Homer in George Chapman's craggy Elizabethan translation. He and a friend had sat up virtually the whole night, with a borrowed folio (large-size) copy, and then Keats went home—but not to bed, far too excited to sleep. He had known Homer only by reputation, before; now, for the first time, he felt that he knew something of Homer as a poet—and so he wrote the sonnet, of which I've quoted only the first four lines, and sent a copy to his friend's lodgings, where it was found lying on the table when the friend finally came down to breakfast.

> Bright star, would I were steadfast as thou art—
> Not in lone splendour hung aloft the night,
> And watching, with eternal lids apart,
> Like Nature's patient sleepless Eremite,   [Eremite-hermit]
> The moving waters at their priestlike task . . .

This is the beginning of another sonnet by Keats, written only five years later, but written on board ship to Italy, traveling to the warm south of Europe in a last desperate attempt to beat off the tuberculosis that soon killed him.

This was Keats' last poem. A few weeks later he was in Italy, writing in a letter that "if I were well there is enough in this Port of Naples to fill a quire [24 large sheets] of paper—but . . . I do not feel in the world." Five weeks later he wrote, with rare and utterly final perception, that "the knowledge of contrast, feeling for light and shade, all that information (primitive sense) necessary for a poem, are great enemies to . . . recovery." He did not write poetry again, and he did not recover. Where the poem about Homer bursts with vitality, beats with the pulse of excitement, the 1820 sonnet is weary, surfeited, heavy. "I have an habitual feeling," he wrote in his last letter home, "of my real life having passed, and that I am leading a posthumous existence."

The point is not that the reader of poetry needs to be a reader, also, of poets' biographies, or of critical histories, but only that poetry proceeds pretty directly out of life. There is no such thing, in that sense, as a "pure" poet, a poet who writes without connection to the actual experience of his time and his place.

> In vain, in vain—the all-composing Hour
> Resistless falls: The Muse obeys the Power.
> She comes! she comes! the sable Throne behold
> Of *Night* Primaeval, and of *Chaos* old!
> Before her, *Fancy*'s gilded clouds   [Fancy-Imagination]
>   decay,
> And all its varying rainbows die away.
> Wit shoots in vain its momentary fires,
> The meteor drops, and in a flash expires. . . .
> Thus at her felt approach, and secret might,
> *Art* after *Art* goes out, and all is Night.

This is Alexander Pope, writing about 1728. The poem is called *The Dunciad*, and it is a long, detailed, savage attack on bad writing and worse writers. At the end of the poem, however, Pope pretends that Dullness has in spite of everything been victorious—"She [Dullness] comes! she comes!" —and Fancy (or Imagination) dies, wit dies, Art itself dies. These lines have such energy, such passion, and evoke so wildly a scene of desperate fireworks succeeded by dismal darkness, that it is sometimes hard to keep in mind their comparatively petty origin. Bad writing matters, surely; it is better that writing be good than bad, and society (as well as other writers) is the beneficiary if it is good. But does a horror of bad writing really justify so intense, so dramatic a scene as Pope gives us? The answer is that the question is irrelevant: Pope establishes that scene, and it does not matter, on the highest level, from what material he works. Provided that a poet works honestly, deeply with the material he has, we cannot attack him for choosing that material rather than something different. There are reasons, yes, for Pope's choice of subject: his body was deformed from birth, and much of his life was spent with books. In addition to the normal writer's loathing for meretricious hackwork, Pope had his own greater absorption in the world of print—and he had, too, a considerable interest in hitting back at the many hack writers who had hit out at him, always savagely and sometimes with the kind of horrible, dull brutality that frequently marks the unintelligent mind. Pope had, in short, good cause, and he had a passionate involvement, and (with the addition of poetic ability of the first order) that is all you need to produce great poetry.

> I would to heaven that I were so much clay,
>   As I am blood, bone, marrow, passion, feeling—
> Because at least the past were passed away—
>   And for the future—(but I write this reeling,
> Having got drunk exceedingly today,
>   So that I seem to stand upon the ceiling)
> I say—the future is a serious matter—
> And so—for God's sake—hock and   [hock-white wine]
>   soda-water!

One of Pope's most fervent admirers, Lord Byron, wrote this on the back of the manuscript of his gorgeously funny long poem, *Don Juan*. I defy anyone to say what the subject of these lines is, at least in less than a complex paragraph. There are two deliberately opposed tones working at the same time, one apparently philosophical and sober, the other inebriate and totally indifferent to philosophy and its questions. The inebriate tone prevails, which I suppose is designed to say something—but nothing very precise or particularized. And yet these are, for me, some of the most memorable lines in all English poetry. They have so intense a joy, so exuberant a vitality, that I find them irresistible, perpetually appealing. I am often tempted to treat them like a kind of little play and act them out: they are much better writing for the stage than Byron produced in his plays, for the simple reason that this *is* Byron, this is the man himself, and in his best good-humored form. (Like all wits, Byron had a vicious side; it does not show in this stanza.) People who knew him described him as being just this sort of mercurial, charismatic man. Best of all, we have a kind of portrait, in his letters, which neatly matches this scribbled stanza. Writing to Thomas Moore, in 1817, he starts as one writer to another: "Have you seen ——'s book of poesy? and, if you have seen it, are you not delighted with it? And have you—I really cannot go on. There is a pair of great black eyes looking over my shoulder, like the angel leaning over St. Matthew's, in the old frontispiece to the Evangelists—so that I must turn and answer them instead of you." With which the letter ends. And a letter to one of his Italian mistresses, carefully written in English (which she could not read) and on the last page of one of her books, begins: "I have read this book in your garden— my love, you were absent, or else I could not have read it." And after a very sober, very passionate declaration of love, Byron concludes: "But all this is too late. I love you, and you love me—at least, you *say so,* and *act* as if you *did* so, which last is a great consolation in all events. But *I* more than love you, and cannot cease to love you. Think of me, sometimes, when the Alps and the ocean divide us—but they never will, unless you *wish* it." The stanza scribbled on the back of the poet's manuscript, then, is superb poetry because it brings the *man* to life again—and men like Byron are extraordinary in any time, fascinating to know, important to understand. If poetry can give us them, can we possibly complain that it does not give us something else?

The many-sidedness of meaning cannot be exhausted, cannot really be even surrounded, in one book or a dozen. People write poetry with a different voice than they talk prose (just as people sing songs with a different voice), but since—once again—it is all *people*-talk, the diversity is unavoidably as great as the range of human concerns, everything from love to politics, science to war, sociology to religion. Or just plain nonsense, which is something people talk too:

> Once, a fence, with nice big slats
> And space between, all airy fat.
>
> And then, a building-builder came,
> Admired that space, abducted same
>
> And used it, grooved it, piled it high,
> Built a -scraper toward the sky-
>
> The fence stood bare, spaceless, numb,
> Stupid as dawn, naked, dumb

And ugly as sin. Impossible. Ugh.
The City squashed it like a noxious bug.

But the building-builder collected his fee
And sailed for Afri- or Ameri-key.

This is "The Fence," by Christian Morgenstern, an early twentieth-century German fantasist who did not like his poems to be called "nonsense." (The translation is my own.) It's not hard to see why: there are implicit (but not *explicit*) values and attitudes expressed by the poem, attitudes which fit very well with Morgenstern's more direct pronouncements. "Above all, our [German] language is 'middle class,' in the middle of our road. To drive it to one side or the other, or even off the road, is the noblest task of the future." The closest thing to Morgenstern, in English, is Lewis Carroll: "Twinkle, twinkle, little bat!/ How I wonder what you're at!/ Up above the world you fly,/ Like a tea-tray in the sky." Or:

'Twas brillig, and the slithy toves
    Did gyre and gimble in the wabe:
All mimsy were the borogoves,
    And the mome raths outgrabe.

"Beware the Jabberwock, my son!
    The jaws that bite, the claws that catch!
Beware the Jubjub bird, and shun
    The frumious Bandersnatch!"

Both Morgenstern and Lewis Carroll are approaching *meaning,* to the extent that they are approaching it at all, sideways, like a scuttling crab. But that, too, is a fundamental part of poetry: it is true, as Ezra Pound has said, that poetry should be at least as well written as prose, but it is also true that anything which can be said as well, or even in the same way, in prose, has no business being said in poetry. If the melody of a song is in no significant way distinguishable from ordinary speech, is it in fact "melody"? If a painting could achieve *exactly* the verisimilitude of a photograph, would it still be a painting, or only an imitation of a photograph, done by devious and rather silly means?

There is always at least something indirect about poetry, and the indirection is basic. Prose tries to be as direct as possible. When prose cannot help itself, it slides into indirectness, but only incidentally, only ornamentally, never basically—or else we have somehow crossed the line between poetry and prose. (Whatever that line is, and wherever it is drawn.) Thomas Wolfe's *Look Homeward, Angel* has an epigraph (a quotation at the beginning of a book), composed by Wolfe himself, which begins " . . . a stone, a leaf, an unfound door; of a stone, a leaf, a door," and ends, "O lost, and by the wind grieved ghost, come back again." The book is a novel, a prose work; the epigraph is spread on the page like prose. But has it perhaps crossed the line into poetry? (Someone once took selected passages from Wolfe's novels, arranged them as poetry, and published them as a collection of Wolf's "poems." The book's critical reception was good.) There would in any case be little argument, I think, if I said that Wolfe's is "poetic" prose. Or if I said that the following, from Matthew Arnold's rather silly memorial to a dead dog, "Kaiser Dead," is pretty prosy stuff:

> Six years ago I brought him down,
> A baby dog, from London town;
> Round his small throat of black and brown
> A ribbon blue,
> And vouched by glorious renown
> A dachshound true.

This has rhyme to a more obvious degree than does prose; it has nineteenth-century poetic inversions ("a ribbon blue," instead of the normal English "a blue ribbon"—because, plainly, "ribbon" does not rhyme with "true," and "blue" does); it has the inflated poetic diction that Wordsworth hated and on which much bad poetry thrives ("vouched by glorious renown"). It is bad poetry: that I assume as absolutely axiomatic. (I would refuse to talk to anyone who maintained, seriously, that this was anything other than *bad* poetry!) But surely one of the chief reasons for its badness is its lack of indirection—or, put in different terms, its close resemblance to prose.

This can be a matter of rhythm, too, as well as language. The most important thing, the one indispensable thing, for any poet, is a good ear—the ability to make language musical. A good ear alone will not make good poetry, but a bad ear makes good poetry impossible. Gregory Corso and Lawrence Ferlinghetti illustrate this beautifully:

> (1) Should I get married? Should I be good?
> Astound the girl next door
> with my velvet suit and faustus hood?
> Don't take her to movies but to cemeteries
> tell all about werewolf bathtubs and forked clarinets

> then desire her and kiss her and all the preliminaries
> and she going just so far and I understanding why
> not getting angry . . .

(2) I am leading a quiet life
    in Mike's Place every day
    watching the champs
    of the Dante Billiard Parlor
    and the French pinball addicts.
    I am leading a quiet life
    on lower East Broadway.
    I am an American. . . .

Excerpt number one is by Gregory Corso, the first lines of a nice poem called "Marriage." Nice, yes—but good poetry? It's not just that Corso writes a deliberately flat style, for excerpt number two, which is the opening of Ferlinghetti's "Autobiography," is flatter still—but number two has the swing, the *authority,* of fine poetry. If you read both these passages aloud (and poetry should almost always be read aloud, to be fully understood), Corso seems, really, to have no rhythm at all. His lines just spill on and on, like the talk—and talk is prose, not poetry—on which they're based. His lines are also based, but erroneously, on Walt Whitman and Allen Ginsberg, both of whom have good poetic ears and so can make even their bad lines— and they both have lots of bad lines—jump and swing. Ferlinghetti has given his lines a cadence, has shaped their rhythm so that form and substance are fully one, so that the medium *is* the message. Corso makes sporadic use of rhyme, here, to tighten things up (good/hood, cemeteries/ preliminaries), but it doesn't work well, the rhymes are not very apparent and they don't do much. Ferlinghetti can write what we often call "free verse," verse without such traditional devices as a predetermined metrical pattern and a predetermined formal structure, and can make it work, because his lines take on a shape of their own, have a rhythm of their own. (It's worth noting, too, how uneven, how cluttered Corso's diction is, and how clean and consistent is Ferlinghetti's.) Corso, in short, is constantly straining, yelling, jumping, gesticulating, because his verse cannot sustain itself. He cannot afford to strive for a contained, even tone. He is, in a sense, writing prose without knowing it; the struggle to turn prose into poetry, by *external* devices, is bound to fail. Good prose is superb stuff, neither worse nor better than poetry, but very different. And well-balanced prose also requires a good ear—

but an ear tuned to different melodies. It's simply a matter
of knowing what you're up to, a matter of being honest
with yourself and with your readers. Corso is not deceitful,
I think, but only self-deceiving. We are better off un-
deceived.

A poet's meaning can be political—why not?—just as
easily as it can be anything else that matters. We have lost
the particular literary situation in which political poetry
flourishes; political poetry which is poetry, not doggerel,
seems rather strange to us, today, though it was common
enough in the eighteenth and even in the early nineteenth
century. The tradition ran into the ground, in our culture,
at about the time Queen Victoria ascended the throne. In
Vietnamese culture, however, the tradition has never fal-
tered:

(1) The road was well guarded, its thousand houses
        stayed shut and silent;
    Officials of all seven ranks attended in full
        uniform—
    And a white-haired soldier, too,
    Who kept telling tales of Nguyen-   [Nguyen-phong-a
        phong.   past era of unbroken peace]

(2) Failures, see him now!
    Ah, the joy of final graduation.
    On the high chair the French *dame* raises her
        mallard's arse
    And in the courtyard, below, the new graduate
    Lifts his dragon's head.

(3) Tsing Ming, and it   [Tsing Ming-a festival time]
    Drizzles on.
    "Freedom, where's freedom?" The jailer points
    To the governor's house, far, far away.

(The translations are my own.) Poem number one was
written in the thirteenth century, number two in the nineteenth, and number three by Ho Chi Minh. All of them
indicate how naturally, how delicately, poets can speak of
political matters. Delicacy is of course not required: the
plays of Aristophanes are quite often savage political as-
saults, and the contemporary German writer, Bertolt
Brecht, once snarled *"Erst kommt die Fressen, dann kommt
die Moral,* First you stuff your face, then you talk about
morality." And the entire four-part "concluding chapter"

in Brecht's biting *Manual of Piety* (1927), titled "Against Seduction," goes like this:

1)
Don't let the bastards seduce you!
There's no way back.
Daylight's cracked
With dark, the night wind's loose at you,
And morning's been hit with an axe.

2)
Don't let the bastards screw you!
Life's just a couple of drops:
Swallow everything due you!
The stuff will stick in your crop
When they tell you it's time to stop!

3)
Don't let the bastards stone you!
There's not much time!
The righteous can rot in their slime!
Don't let them act like they own you!
Life's a damned short loan!

4)
Don't let the bastards seduce you,
Grind you, shove you down!
What in hell can you lose?
You die and you lie in the ground,
Then nothing. No harps. No crown.

(The translation is my own.) The contrast between this pungent violence and the carefully contained passion of Vietnam is not so great, I think, as the contrast between either the Vietnamese or the German poets, on the one hand, and, say, Robert Lowell. Lowell has, as I write these words, the largest reputation of any living American poet. He has been involved in a good many political activities, made a good many political gestures and statements. That he should write political poetry is only to be expected—but that it should be as tepid, as grimly uninteresting as it is, *that* is harder to take:

From the first cave, the first farm, the first sage,
inalienable our human right to murder—
"We must get used," they say, "to the thought of guns;
we must get used to seeing guns; we must
get used to using guns." Guns too are mortal. Guns
failed Che Guevara, Marie Antoinette,

Leon Trotsky, the children of the Tsar:
chivalrous ornaments to power. Tom Paine said
Burke pitied the plumage and forgot the dying bird. . . .

This is by no means the worst of the many, many political
poems in *Notebook 1967–68*. One titled "For Eugene Mc-
Carthy," for example, begins: "I love you so. . . . Gone?
Who will swear you wouldn't/ have done good to the country, the fulfillment wouldn't/ have done good to you . . ."
(The ellipsis—three dots, usually indicating that something
has been left out—after the words "I love you so" is Lowell's. It does not here indicate an omission.) This is
heavy, portentous stuff, deeply uninteresting. There is a
good deal of lively quasi-doggerel on political subjects,
these days, and it is much more interesting than Lowell's
flat pomposities. But is it *poetry*?

This book is an introduction to poetry, not an introduction to American culture: I cannot even begin to account
for these failures, here. But any discussion of political
poetry designed to be read in the United States must, I
think, pretty much rely—as I have relied—on poetry from
other cultures. (Alan Dugan does have one very beautiful
political poem, in his book *Poems 2:* "Riding Song for a
Semi-Feudal Army, for Glubb Pasha, for Tortured Colo-
nels." But this poem is forty lines long, and is too tightly
woven to be quoted only in an excerpt. Nor has Dugan
maintained this level: the political poems in his most recent
book, *Poems 3,* are unfortunately about as bad as Lowell's,
though fortunately they are a smaller proportion of the
volume.)

One more *way* of meaning needs to be mentioned in this
first chapter: allegory. Essentially, allegory is a straightforward device, in which the poet substitutes a symbol or
set of symbols for whatever reality it is that he is writing
about. The fairy queen of Spenser's *Faerie Queene* is both
Glory and Queen Elizabeth I; the Red Cross Knight of
Holiness is the Anglican Church; the Virgin Una is truth,
or the true religion, and so on. For a sustained and full-
length allegory, of course, a writer needs to be able to
articulate a complex and consistent set of symbols: it's
no good veering back and forth, one minute naturalistic, the
next allegorical. (Unless, that is, the writer's purpose is
comic.) Full-length allegories have been written in both
prose and poetry: outstanding prose examples, in English

literature, are the morality play *Everyman* (fifteenth century) and John Bunyan's *Pilgrim's Progress* (1678). Franz Kafka is I think the leading allegorist of the twentieth century. The allegorical way of meaning is not terribly popular, today, in spite of Kafka and others—but it was once of major importance, in good part because Christianity itself saw man's life on earth as a kind of preliminary allegory, the meaning of which would be either salvation or damnation. Nor does allegory require full-length exposition:

> This world a-hunting is:
> The prey, poor man; the
>   Nimrod fierce is death;   [Nimrod-a "mighty hunter"]
> His speedy greyhounds are
> Lust, sickness, envy, care,
> Strife that ne'er falls amiss,
> With all those ills which haunt us while we breathe.
> Now if, by chance, we fly
> Of these the eager chase,
> Old age with stealing pace
> Casts up his nets, and there we panting die.

This is "Madrigal 4" by William Drummond, a contemporary of John Donne but in emotional make-up something of an anachronism in his own time. His allegory—life as a chase, in which Death hunts, and man is hunted—is complete. Some of the details are simply and barely presented, rather than elaborated: "His speedy greyhounds are/ Lust, sickness, envy, care . . . ." But Drummond could rely on many prior years of just such associations; his readers would automatically fill in the details Drummond chooses to omit. The heart of the poem, to me, is the sudden switch from chase-metaphor to fishing-metaphor, at the end, with the lovely image of "there we panting die." It is not only brilliantly effective poetry, however: it also takes a different religious allegory, the notion of Peter the fisherman as the fisher of souls, and deliberately stands it on its head. Instead of the soul being caught by Good, that is, and thereby transported to eternal bliss, Drummond shows us the soul/fish being caught by a force not at all good, namely Death. He does *not* say, please note, that the soul thereupon goes to Hell: he is indeed quite careful not to say this, since he is a very Christian poet. Rather, the inversion of the "fisher of souls" metaphor serves as a warning: be careful, he suggests, or else. All of this makes the poem quietly subtle—and also gives renewed interest to the fairly stock presentation of the "life as chase" metaphor.

And note, too, how easily a discussion of allegory becomes a discussion of metaphor. In one sense, allegory *is* a kind of metaphor, but an extended metaphor of greater than usual complexity. It is as if, in a sense, the poet takes one of his basic building blocks—metaphorical expression —and enlarges it, gives it narrative as well as imagistic significance.

But we still have to discuss metaphor.

CHAPTER TWO: What Poetry Does: Metaphor

The chief difference between allegory and metaphor is that allegory is systematic: it tries to present either an entire world-view or, at the least, an idea of considerable scope and significance—religious, political, sociological, sexual, philosophical. The content matters much less than the approach. But metaphor is less ambitious: it tries to present only a single new perspective, to illuminate only a single notion. "As flies to wanton boys are we to the gods./ They kill us for their sport," says the blinded old Duke of Gloucester, in Shakespeare's *King Lear*. Hamlet tells us that "the native hue of resolution/ Is sicklied o'er with the pale cast [tinge, color] of thought." When Othello, still flushed with pride, orders a brawl to stop, he declares: "Keep up your bright swords, for the dew will rust them." In none of these lines is the metaphor really concerned with its apparent substance. Gloucester is not concerned with the cruelty of small boys to flies: he is not arguing for the prevention of cruelty to flies, but presenting a bitter, cynical view of man's relationship to the superhuman. Hamlet is not mixing paint, or reacting to a new portrait, but commenting on how thought, which is "pale," bleaches away the basic vitality (metaphorically, the "native hue") of decision. And Othello is not worried about the state of the combatants' swords, nor does he really believe that the damp night air ("dew") will actually rust them. The "brightness," here, is a moral thing: the swords will be ruined, stained by being exposed, by being used in the way intended. By inference, too, the stain will carry over to the men who wield the swords. *Their* honor will also be rusted. (Note that swords, when used, produce blood, which then dries to something closely resembling rust. This plain but secondary fact reinforces the strength of the metaphor, though it is not necessary to it.)

34

Because metaphor is inherently indirect, and poetry is also inherently (though not invariably) indirect, it makes perfectly good sense for poets to make constant use of metaphor. And they do: it sits at the center of almost all poetic expression, in almost all languages, and in all times. Some styles of poetry emphasize it more or less, some poets emphasize it more or less, but it is almost always there. Not that it is essential to have metaphor in order to have poetry. There is, I think, nothing that is absolutely essential to poetry, except perhaps musicality—which I would not like to have to define, though I know perfectly well, for myself, what it is, and which poems and poets have it, and which do not. But even if it is not essential, metaphor is used by poets in an enormous number of ways, and for an enormous number of purposes. When Andrew Marvell wants to indicate to his "Coy Mistress" that, given an infinity of time, he could let his love go forward with infinite patience, he tells her that "My vegetable love should grow/ Vaster than empires, and more slow." A "vegetable" love is, plant-like, in no terribly great hurry; Marvell turns his love into this kind of growth, and then elaborates the metaphor by explaining that even at this excruciatingly slow pace his love is capable of monstrous size, "vaster than empires." And then a second metaphor is grafted onto the first: since empires do not "grow" overnight, any more than vegetables do, Marvell adds that his "vegetable love" will expand "more slow" than even an empire. The sense of serpentine movement, ponderous and stagnating, is beautifully and wittily conveyed—because all the time we are fully aware that this is both hypothetical and ridiculous. No lover, and no belovèd, have in fact an infinity of time. Marvell goes on: "But at my back I always hear/ Time's winged chariot hurrying near . . . . The grave's a fine and private place,/ But none I think do there embrace."

> Green grape, and you refused me.
> Ripe grape, and you sent me packing.
> Must you deny me a bite of your raisin?

This anonymous ancient Greek poet, here translated by Dudley Fitts (who ranks with Ezra Pound and Arthur Waley as one of the very great translators of our time), has built his entire poem on one fascinatingly simple metaphor. The lover in fact often wishes to "eat" his belovèd; much of the language of love involves some kind of food imagery. You eat food; fruit, which is a kind of food, begins green and then ripens, and then dries and rots—and there is the poem, all built into a single extended metaphor. He knew her when she was young ("green grape"), wanted her, and did not get her. He knew her when she had matured, grown from a girl into a woman ("ripe grape"), and the story was still the same. He wants her still, though now she is old and withered ("raisin"), but she still turns him down. Why, he asks? All he wants is "a bite"—that is, he no longer wants the whole thing, he no longer hopes to fully or permanently possess her, but just to transiently enjoy a bit of what there is left to enjoy. And what he wants a "bite" of is only a "raisin," dried out and worth virtually nothing. Why then is she still so scornful?

This tightly worked-out metaphor expresses a number of things, all at the same time. There is, first of all, the desirability, the consumability of the beloved. And then there is the sense of how this desirability, and the persona's desire, has lasted over time, through the long and frustrating passage from "green grape" all the way down to "raisin." The sense of the steady, heavy march of time is also pressed on us, through this natural cycle of growth and decay. And more: by making the sexual "food" a single grape, to start with, and a single raisin, at the end, the poet also comments on the comparative unimportance—indeed, in cosmic terms, the utter triviality—of what the belovèd has all the time refused him. There is even some sense, though not fully articulated, of how *he* is reasonable, long-suffering and rational, while *she* is arrogant, intensely selfish, and altogether less reasonable, less rational, perhaps even more creature-like than—in the fullest and best sense—human. But this is, as I say, not entirely clear—even though it fits nicely into a very probable notion, for an ancient Greek poet, about the rationality of the male and the irrationality of the intellectually inferior female. (The rational party, in this view, can admire and even passionately desire the beauty of the irrational party, but always understands, at the same time, the relative worth and standing of the two, in any higher view of things.)

Except for the obvious fact that such subtlety, such perfection of a dazzlingly simple technique is an esthetic delight in itself, I have *not* been talking about the esthetics of this poem. I'd like to make this very clear: drooling over the poetic beauties of poetry is not either the intellectual purpose or the emotional orientation of this book. As a poet, as a reader of poetry, and as a teacher of poetry, I take a large and enthusiastic delight in poetry, but I do not feel that delight can be taught. To use (appropriately enough) a metaphor: I can teach you something about color harmony and balance, something about composition, something about emphasis and contrast and the general use of line, but I cannot teach you to like Picasso. With what I teach you, you can perhaps teach yourself to like his painting, having first come to understand it better. To drop the metaphor (but also to extend it): I have talked about *meaning*, we are now talking about *metaphor*, and we will shortly talk about *rhythm and music, contrast and balance, precision and neatness*, and about *control and form*. Each of these is (or can be) a component of a poem; each of these can be savored for its own sake, and after a time as part of a complex whole which utilizes many components. But until you are at least partly sensitized to the components, it seems to me rather silly to talk about "appreciation." Pleasure is not an empty-headed concept; enjoyment is not trivial, is not a matter of gushing, of rhetoric and verbal pyrotechnics. Pleasure is a basic, a very real human emotion, and it must be founded, like any other emotion which is to be meaningful, on something quite solid. When a boy loves a girl in the way that too many people gush meaninglessly about poetry, marriage is followed by either divorce or disaster.

Let me also point out that I am not arguing, nor have I argued, nor will I argue, that poetry will save your soul, or improve your chances of reaching Heaven, or clean out your kidneys. Poetry is poetry: it does what it does—and that being the subject of this chapter, I will return to it.

Ben Jonson, Shakespeare's great contemporary, is an elegant and musical poet of perhaps overly-controlled passion. But when his young children died, as too many of them did, he became distinctly less controlled and more passionate—and his metaphorical expression kept pace:

> Rest in soft peace, and, asked, say *here doth lie*
> *Ben Jonson his best piece of poetry.*
> For whose sake, henceforth, all his vows be such,
> As what he loves may never like too much.

"Poetry," which Jonson spelled "poetrie" and pronounced as a three-syllable word rhyming with "die, lie, buy," and so on, is here the gentlest, deftest of metaphors. A poet writes (or makes, or produces, or fabricates) poetry. This is the literal fact from which the metaphor starts. The poet being also, as I have said several times, a man, he makes (or produces, or fabricates) other things as well, children included. The connotations of the word "poetry" are excellent: the *O.E.D.* (*Oxford English Dictionary on Historical Principles*) records that by 1581 it meant "the expression of beautiful or elevated thought, imagination, or feeling, in appropriate language." The connotations of the word "son" (the title to this poem, of which I have quoted only the last four lines, is "On my first son") are also excellent. What Jonson has done is to cross the two, building the jointure on the functional sameness of the poet's role in each situation: that is, the poet makes the poem and he also makes the child. And this jointure adds the glowing connotations of "poetry" to those of "son," producing a very powerful composite.

There is of course more at work. A poet often writes, and Jonson certainly wrote, with one eye on his fame in days to come. In that sense, his "best piece of poetry" matters a very great deal. But a son is both a product intended for the future and at the same time is posterity itself, is the future. The *man's* loss, when his son dies, is made more poignant by shifting it to the unfamiliar context of the *poet's* loss of a poem. And then, we are also aware that this is Jonson writing about his own son; the metaphor is in that sense not a metaphor at all, but the literal truth, for Jonson is here man and is poet, both at once, and both together aching with pain and grief. Finally, since Jonson is (as he writes this poem) still alive, and will surely write more poetry, the unqualified assertion that the dead child is his "best" poem nullifies any possibility of the future producing its equal, let alone its superior. This gives the metaphor a haunting finality, and gives us some sense of how wonderful the child was, in his poet-father's eyes.

> We are the hollow men
> We are the stuffed men
> Leaning together
> Headpiece filled with straw.

This is the beginning of T. S. Eliot's "The Hollow Men," a poem of deep and self-lacerating despair. The poet's ache is, here, of a very different sort, both more generalized and more enduring. That is, this is an ache which he feels, but which he does not feel only for himself. Nor is it an ache which is likely to ebb. Time will ease the pain of Ben Jonson's loss, which is a particular one. But time will only extend, or prolong, the pain of Eliot's realization. He expresses this by the flat but by no means simple metaphor of the first line, "We are the hollow men." "Hollow" operates on two basic levels, as a description of our internal state (spiritually-empty-hollow), and as a picture of our actual physical state (three-dimensionally-hollow). On either level he pictures our state as a fully developed and continuing one: "we *are*," not "such-and-such has *made* us be," or "we have *become*." The assertion is flat, seamless, and in context unarguable. And it is reinforced by line two, "We are the stuffed men." Literally, one cannot be both hollow and stuffed at the same time, but there is no question of a clash. We are "hollow" in exactly the same sense in which we are "stuffed"—the sense, that is, in which we as humans lack a human core, a human center. Whether we are literally empty, or only empty in that we have stuffing of a nonhuman sort inside us, to give us the appearance of a substantiality we have never really had, it does not matter. The important thing is, as the root metaphor tells us, that we are human shells, devoid of spirituality, empty of everything that makes human beings truly human. The insistent repetition of "we," in lines one and two, leads to the ironic "togetherness" of line three. We are all in it "together," yes, but we might almost as well be alone, for all the good that we do each other. Like scarecrows in a field, leaning on our supporting sticks, leaning in the wind, our "headpieces"—a carefully calculated word, designed to further dehumanize us—are "filled with straw," not with brains. If we had brains, Eliot suggests, we would be something very different; we would somehow face our predicament and think our way through it. The fact that, as he sees us, we refuse to face our situation, refuse to even try to improve it, is proof enough that we lack the capacity for human reaction, for thought and feeling. The puppet-and-scarecrow imagery is exactly right for his purpose: this is "intellectual" poetry, founded on intellectual perceptions and anxious to communicate them, but it does not need to use "intellectual formulations." Eliot does not say: We are spiritually empty people, unable to feel, unable to think. That would be an accurate prose summation of what he has said—but the prose summation is, as I hope I have made perfectly clear, in no way the same thing as the poetry which it summarizes.

It is important to realize that there is no such thing, in fact, as a prose paraphrase of a metaphor—any more than there can be a translation which is identical to the translated original, or a critical analysis which is the same as the painting or the poem or the sonata or the statue which it analyzes. There is so much built-in meaning, on so many levels (lexical as well as musical, associative as well as direct and primary), that a prose paraphrase is more like a tourist guidebook than the thing actually on display. Only the thing itself is the thing itself; only the poem is the poem, only the metaphor is the metaphor.

One way of talking about the difference between an idea and a metaphor—which both expresses the idea and at the same time says things, often many things, about the context and effect and significance of the idea—is to say that an idea (prose) is "intellectual" and a metaphor (poetry) is "nonintellectual." "Nonintellectual" is however not a very good way of saying what I mean. "Nonrational" would be better, except that it suggests "irrationality," which is not what I mean at all—and also ignores the fact that there is no one way of being rational. We usually assume, and our usual language supports us in this belief, that rationality is of a piece, is unitary and always the same. Two and two are four; the shortest distance between two points is a straight line; parallel lines never meet; and so on. The trouble is that although two and two are in fact four, in some methods of discourse, in others they are not. (The poet E. E. Cummings once titled a book "Is 5," to assert this. He meant: two and two can just as well be five.) Your girl friend criticizes your driving, or your father, and what she really means is "Do you love me? I'm scared that you don't—and so I'll hit you first, before you can hurt me." A child asks, "How many children in —— are deserted by their mothers and fathers?" What he means to ask is, however, "Will *you* desert *me?*" This is not logic in the usual sense of the word, but neither is it illogical. The concept of "two and two is four" depends, for its validity, on the assumption of a neat Euclidian world in which every "two" is like every other "two," and all the relationships between the entities of that world are fixed into airtight categories. The distance from a "two" to a "five," say, must therefore always be the same, and every "eight" must be twice as large as every "four."

The world of human beings, as everyone in the twentieth century should know, is simply not like that. Our categories are not always the same, nor are they always the same with relationship to each other. In 1941 the Germans were "bad" and the Russians were "good." In 1970 the Germans are "good" and the Russians are "bad." Before President Sukarno was deposed, Indonesia was a "bad" country. It now has a pro-Western government, and so it has suddenly become a "good" country. These categorizations do have meaning, surely, and they do express something; they are not empty verbalizations. But neither are they hard and fast categories, quantifiable in precise terms. Were the Germans 100 per cent bad, when they were bad? Or perhaps 87 per cent bad? Were the Russians more "good," when they were good, than the Germans are, now that *they* have become "good"? The question is vaguely idiotic: one does not think of these categorizations in such precise terms. Which is precisely the point: human relationships are not susceptible to objective formularizations, constant and unchanging. Parallel lines *do* meet (as Einstein has demonstrated), under the right conditions. The shortest distance between two points may be a terribly circuitous route. If you want something from someone, how often is it best to walk right up to him and demand what you desire? That is the shortest route, clearly. It is plainly not the best route. You are more likely to succeed if you move slowly and cautiously and circuitously, if you try to take into account all the other man's individual quirks and peculiarities, if you try to wait until exactly the right moment, and so on.

Poetry knows these things intuitively. It understands that to say, in bald prose, "We are spiritually empty people, unable to feel, unable to think," may be *clear,* but it will not very likely be effective. Poetry knows that people do not think only with their minds, that their bodies and their guts are also deeply involved. "I hate my father," says someone. "Yeah, he's a bastard, your father." "Shut up! Don't you dare insult my father." Baseball players try to "hit-'em-where-they-ain't"; football players try to move around or to avoid an opponent; generals try to invade where enemy fortifications are weakest, even if this means a longer attack route. The blunt, full-speed-ahead-and-damn-the-torpedoes approach can sometimes work. More often, it produces a Charge of the Light Brigade, stupidly conceived, maniacally executed, in which nothing is accomplished but the destruction of many good people. Poetry, as I keep insisting, is human activity; it operates, in this sense, exactly as a good athlete or a good general or a good parent must, by suitable indirections. And metaphor is the chief of these indirections. Eliot's puppet-scarecrow image is more effective than the bald prose summary, "We are spiritually empty people," because it needs no preparation, it does not depend on a context being established for it. *It makes its own context.* That is, good poetry creates a kind of small world, and allows us to penetrate and experience that world. We can and usually do receive "prose" ideas from that penetration, from that experience, but we receive and experience more as well. "Genuine poetry can communicate before it is understood," says Eliot, in his essay on Dante. "I was passionately fond of certain French poetry long before I could have translated two verses of it correctly."

Perhaps because my own early training was in physics, I like to think of poetry—which is after all as natural a force as a bullet fired from a gun, or a flying buttress holding up a cathedral wall, or a man slamming into a tree—as working in terms of what physics calls "vectors." That is, in deciding what the result of certain pressures and forces will be, physics analyzes the situation in terms of the mass and velocity of each pressure, of each force. The stronger pressures will have more effect, but the weaker pressures also must be taken into account: it is the *sum* of *all* the pushing, shoving vectors which matters, not the particular force and weight of each individual vector. In physics, of course, you can in theory always identify and measure the individual vectors, so that the resultant is (again, in theory) always knowable. The vectors of poetry are harder to control, analytically; some of them slip away like wet tadpoles as you try to catch and measure them. And yet the poem *is*. You may not be able to reduce it to its individual vectors, but that is your failure, not its. The kind of analysis which physics permits, that is, is not successful in trying to analyze poetry. And what I draw from all this—as any student who has studied poetry with me could confirm—is a distinction between such "linear" processes as physics deals in, and the "nonlinear" processes of poetry. Both poetry and physics are logical but—like men and women, often—logical each in its own way. Neither linear nor nonlinear logic is superior. Neither variety comes from a different source, both are human, deeply human. But they deal with different materials, and deal with them in different ways. Physics and other linear approaches are concerned, basically, with the external world, the world of measures and quantities. Poetry, and such other nonlinear approaches as music and painting, have not turned their back on the external world, but they are often in touch, also, with those less accessible, usually determinedly *unconscious* centers of our being which "are such stuff as dreams are made on." And metaphor, more than any other component of poetry, draws on this nonlinear world, this internal world where "two" is not two, and the next "two" is something still different, and the resultant of these two "two's" is—whatever it happens to be, ten or forty or zero. Or minus twelve.

To return to T. S. Eliot: "We are spiritually empty people" is conscious, clear, *linear*. "We are the hollow men/ We are the stuffed men" is at least partly emotive, associative rather than assertive, and to that extent *nonlinear*. "He's a rat," which is a very elementary metaphor, cannot be a linear statement, since (as I define it) a linear statement must formulate everything there is to formulate, and must not involve us in emotive imprecisions. (I am *not* saying, please understand, that poetry is necessarily harder to follow, or more obscure, and certainly not that it is inferior. I will come back to this, in the next chapter.) The identity between a man and a rat is inherently nonlinear; no man is in fact a rat, and no rat is in fact a man. We can make an *association* between two things that we know, logically (*linear*-logically), are not the same. This association does not assert identity, but only informs us about some kinds of *similarities*. On this level, the art of metaphor is the art of perceiving relationships, the art of reporting those perceptions from the inside, from the context in which the poet sees them operating. "Here doth lie/ Ben Jonson his best piece of poetry" is Jonson reporting back to us, his readers, from that world of mixed emotion and thought that all art inhabits. (And which, today, art sometimes shares with certain social sciences, especially psychology.) Jonson both reports on his perception and shares with us his feeling about it. Were he to say, in prose summary, "Here lies the dead body of a child I fathered and that I loved so well that he seems to me, a poet, the very best poetry I have ever been capable of," we would be receiving neither perception or feeling, but only an *idea*. Again, I do not mean to denigrate ideas. I mean only to indicate that though there definitely are ideas in poetry, the *primary* business of dealing in ideas lies with other human activities (philosophy, in the purest form, and science, in a more pragmatic context). Or, finally: poetry is not better than philosophy, or science, it is only different. And *vive la différence*.

Metaphor itself is not a single, monolithic phenomenon. (More than twenty years ago, I wrote a hundred-page thesis, determined to prove that metaphor is only metaphor when squarely based on concretions, on *things*. I was dead wrong.) Even at the same moment in history, poets are likely to take very different approaches to imagery. John Donne (1571?–1631) and Ben Jonson (1572–1637) are exact contemporaries; their usual approach to metaphor is sharply and very instructively divergent. Donne usually starts with the object, and builds from that; his generalizations, his abstractions, come on the scene only after the object has first caught our attention to itself, and then redirected our attention, via a metaphorical association, to the abstraction.

> Go and catch a falling star,
>   Get with child a mandrake root,
> Tell me where all past years are,
>   Or who cleft the devil's foot,
> Teach me to hear mermaids singing,
>   Or to keep off envy's stinging,
>   And find
>   What wind   [pronounced to rhyme with "mind"]
> Serves to advance an honest mind.

On first reading, this stanza may seem to be almost a parade of objects: falling stars, mandrake roots (which resemble human beings and have had traditional magical associations), the devil, mermaid-Sirens. Even Time itself is made into a concretion: "Tell me where all past years are." Only at the end of this first stanza of the poem do abstractions appear, and even they can have distinctly physical properties, for Donne. Envy "stings," here, like some mad wasp. Significantly, the final abstraction, the "wind" which is to "advance" (help to prosper, do good things for) an "honest mind," is the vaguest image of all. Donne thus removes the sense of concretion precisely at the moment when he wants to indicate *non*reality. This— the sad plight of honest men in a corrupt world—is really what these lines are about. He does not care about falling stars and mandrake roots, except insofar as they can shed some preliminary light on *this* problem, which is a very human problem. That is, the long list of impossibilities is at least a concrete list, until the impossibility of an honest man doing well in the world is brought up—and that cannot be concrete at all, for it is of all the listed impossibilities the most impossible. You cannot catch falling stars, or conceive a child upon a mandrake root, or know where past time has passed to, or understand the cleft in the devil's foot, or volitionally come to hear mermaids, or be immune from envious men—and whoops! having come to envy, there we are, in the human world, dropped down with a thud. Donne can then move swiftly to the culmination of this stanza, the final impossibility of this particular listing of impossibilites. (The poem as a whole turns out to be about the faithlessness of women, but that is yet another abstraction built upon the preceding particularities: his technique is a consistent one.) There is a special kind of drama, in a series of challenging concretions of this sort. The violent yoking of poetic concretions to a higher pattern and purpose is sometimes called "metaphysical poetry"—but this is not a history of English poetry, and besides, I tend to agree with T. S. Eliot that "Not only is it extremely difficult to define metaphysical poetry, but difficult to decide what poets practise it and in which of their verses."

Yet Donne's technique is clearly different from Ben Jonson's:

> Wouldst thou hear what man can say
> In a little? Reader, stay.
> Underneath this stone doth lie
> As much beauty as could die;
> Which in life did harbor give
> To more virtue than doth live.
> If at all she had a fault,
> Leave it buried in this vault.
> One name was Elizabeth;
> The other, let it sleep with death:
> Fitter, where it died, to tell,
> Than that it lived at all. Farewell!

From the very start, Jonson is at one and the same time more direct and more generalized. The thought comes straight at us; it is not a boldly striking image, which first hits home and then, only afterwards, suggests a meaningful associative meaning. Jonson uses statement as his chief poetic tool. (Where metaphor is "figurative" in approach, statement is "literal." "I hate you" is statement. "You're a rat" is metaphorical.) His language is vigorous and musical, but for the most part there is remarkably little concealed by it. And yet Jonson's little poem is not all statement, not all literal; there are things "concealed," indirectly communicated. Now, if what Donne does when he is indirect is metaphor—"Go and catch a falling star"— then Jonson's indirection is either something different, not metaphor at all, or else metaphor itself is a broader concept than at first appears. "Underneath this stone doth lie/ As much beauty as could die" means that when the unknown woman about whom this little poem was written was dead, and lay buried "underneath this stone," whatever part of a thing as immortal as beauty *could* die had in fact now died. This is surely not literally true: beauty is not an indivisible *thing,* as Jonson suggests, nor is it an imperishable abstraction, and neither is (nor was) this lady the total embodiment of mortal beauty. Jonson is here using, in short, what we might call a fancy, an imaginative projection. His own time called this device a "conceit," an imaginative idea which allowed a poet to express himself in elevated terms, but "in a little" space. The process is actually rather more complex than what goes on in Donne's lines, but it is just as much a way of saying something by way of saying something else. Or, in other terms, it is just as much a metaphor. It is, let me repeat, a very different *way* of saying. The fact that we have to look harder, in order to find what Jonson's metaphor is, does not mean that there is less imaginative projection. It only means that Jonson is doing something different. As I said earlier, Donne is more interested in the process of construction; Jonson is more interested in unraveling a construction which pre-exists. Donne, one can say, is exploring the world, is seeking understanding through a juggling and juxtaposing of relationships between apparently disparate things. But Jonson already knows his world, and wants more to project that knowledge, to filter knowledge down through the objects in his poems. This is a temperamental difference, and it can (and usually does) reach all through a man's life, from art to politics, from sex to theology. (I do not agree with everything in E. M. W. Tillyard's elegant little book, *Poetry Direct and Oblique* (1948), but it is a very good and a very helpful discussion, clear, specific, and continually intelligent. I have been recommending it to undergraduate students for two decades, with excellent results. What Tillyard calls "direct" poetry is work like Ben Jonson's; what he calls "oblique" poetry is work like John Donne's.) *

An "image," as I have been using that word, is pretty much the same thing as a metaphor. When we talk about a poet's "imagery," then, we mean the things, the ideas, the associations, out of which he makes his poems—the material with which he works. These are, it should be said very emphatically, in the ultimate sense volitional. That is, the poet chooses—whether consciously or not is

not for the moment relevant—what he writes about, and
how he writes about what he chooses. And though the
period in which the poet lives is of course important in
shaping these choices, just as his parents are important,
and his health, and the state of his pocketbook, the volitional aspect of the choice is I believe the most important
of all. And to a considerable extent *it* is governed, as I
have indicated, by the poet's *temperament*—which is itself
a complex and ill-definable matter, as much a subject for
psychologists as for people writing books on poetry. Thomas
Hardy, for example, a late Victorian poet (and also of
course a novelist), quite naturally chooses statement in
preference to intense metaphorical expression: "For long
the cruel wish I knew/ That your free heart should ache
for me/ While mine should bear no ache for you . . ."
Poem after poem of his moves in this manner. But when
a Donne-like mood suddenly strikes him, as it does toward
the end of "After a Romantic Day," he can lean in the
other direction:

> The bald steep cutting, rigid, rough,
>   And moon-lit, was enough
> For poetry of place: its weathered face
> Formed a convenient sheet whereon
> The visions of his mind were drawn.

And even Byron, for all his worship of the eighteenth
century, can in the middle of the rattling jollity of his
Don Juan suddenly turn out a stanza like this:

> But words are things, and a small drop of ink,
>   Falling like dew, upon a thought, produces
> That which makes thousands, perhaps millions, think;
>   'Tis strange, the shortest letter which man uses
> Instead of speech, may form a lasting link
>   Of ages; to what straits old Time reduces
> Frail man, when paper—even a rag like this,
> Survives himself, his tomb, and all that's his.

The notion of a drop of ink "falling like dew, upon a
thought," is virtually straight out of the Donne-box. The
whole stanza, indeed, has a startling resemblance to the
tone so characteristic of Donne, and so uncharacteristic
of Byron. But then, even Tennyson, than whom few poets
are less Donne-like, can sometimes write like this:

> What then were God to such as I?
>   'Twere hardly worth my while to choose

> Of things all mortal, or to use
> A little patience ere I die;
>
> 'Twere best at once to sink to peace,
> Like birds the charming serpent draws,
> To drop head-foremost in the jaws
> Of vacant darkness and to cease.

It is not quite so precisely Donne-like as the passage from
Hardy, but "To drop head-foremost in the jaws/ Of vacant
darkness" is clearly more in the Donne tradition than in
the Jonson one.

As I said at the start of this examination of John
Donne and Ben Jonson, metaphor is not a single, monolithic phenomenon. It is a tool: like any other tool it must
fit the craftsman's hand, and not all craftsmen work or
can work in the same way. But most carpenters use a
hammer with some frequency, and most poets use one or
both kinds of metaphor—Donne's or Jonson's—with some
frequency.

But do they have to? Is poetry not poetry without some
kind of metaphor? Samuel Johnson is something of a
test case. Here is a passage from his 1738 imitation of
Juvenal, "London":

> For who would leave, unbribed, Hibernia's [i.e., Ireland]
>   land,
> Or change the rocks of Scotland
>   for the Strand?   [Strand-London street]
> There none are swept by sudden fate away,
> But all whom hunger spares, with age decay:
> Here malice, rapine, accident conspire,
> And now a rabble rages, now a fire;
> Their ambush here relentless ruffians lay,
> And here the fell attorney prowls for prey;
> Here falling houses thunder on your head,
> And here a female atheist talks you dead.

This is not antiseptically free of metaphor. The "fell at-
torney [who] prowls for prey" is obviously analogized to,
and in that sense a metaphor for, some beast of prey,
a wolf most likely. This is not, however, either a very clear
or a very strong metaphor, and the main thrust of the
passage is distinctly not metaphorical. I do not think it is
great poetry (though I happen to enjoy it very much).
It *is* however poetry of a high competence—and why? It
has the rhythm of professional verse, for one thing, the

authoritative sound of an accomplished maker of verbal
music. Beethoven's "Battle Symphony" is not top-drawer
music, it is full of vaguely corny quotations from "God
Save the King" and "La Marseillaise," and the scoring
makes rather cheap use of drums and trumpets—but the
piece remains, for all that, music of high competence,
plainly composed by a man who knows how to put music
together. The question I have asked, remember, is not
about great poetry, but only about poetry: is *poetry* possible without metaphor? Johnson's lines have a clever,
well-trained variety of verbal music (though the last four
lines are perhaps a shade too alike, rhythmically). They
have, too, that special intensity of polarity, of matched
opposites, which is characteristic of the poetry of the
eighteenth century. "And now a rabble rages, now a fire":
it could be argued that this is a kind of concealed metaphor, deliberate coupling of the raging mob with an
uncontrolled fire, which coupling becomes more than just
juxtaposition, which becomes indeed a kind of implicit
comparison. It need not be so seen, however, to have its
effect. "First the fire horn blew, and then Lord Harley
spoke": this is the juxtaposition of ludicrous polarities,
the dignified, respectable man in the top hat slipping fool-
ishly on a banana peel. (Though, again, it can be argued
that juxtaposition is itself only another variety of metaphor.
When the screen shows, first, a man's fist bashing into
another man's stomach, and next shows a ripe watermelon
bursting open, you can say that because these two images
are in series and not in parallel no metaphor has occurred.
You *can* say it, but I would not like to. I see no reason
why metaphor need be always and only in parallel.) The
matched polarities have no metaphorical possibilities, however, in the line "But all whom hunger spares, with age
decay." If hunger spares them, age can have the chance
to decay them: that is, if the Scots and the Irish survive
famine (a nasty observation), they live long (a favorable
observation), they are not subject to such typical urban
deaths as "malice, rapine, accident," or "a rabble," or "a
fire." The line is good poetry because it is balanced, because it has the swing of good verse, and because it has
something fairly intense to say. The "ambush" of the
"relentless ruffians," like the "falling houses" and the "female atheist," are all interpretive description, not in the
least metaphorical. This is Johnson telling it like it is—
and as he feels it to be. We sense his anger, his rage and

frustration—for he loved the London he was writing of, and lived there himself, quite "unbribed."

With the few metaphorical exceptions I have noted, then, I can perhaps summarize by saying that in Johnson's "London" what we hear is a good voice speaking, and speaking artfully, strongly. We listen, because good talk, in a well-modulated voice, is usually worth listening to, is usually enjoyable. It need not have the challenging quality that some good talk *does* have, in order to capture and to hold our attention.

But am I saying, implicitly, that poetry which is relatively free of metaphor is poetry of the second intensity? Consider this:

> O what can ail thee, Knight at arms,
>   Alone and palely loitering?
> The sedge has withered from the lake,   [sedge-rushes]
>   And no birds sing.
>
> O what can ail thee, Knight at arms,
>   So haggard and so woe-begone?
> The squirrel's granary is full,
>   And the harvest's done.
>
> I see a lily on thy brow,
>   With anguish moist and fever dew;
> And on thy cheek a fading rose
>   Fast withereth too.
>
> "I met a lady in the meads,   [meads-meadows]
>   Full beautiful—a fairy's child;
> Her hair was long, her foot was light,
>   And her eyes were wild.
>
> "I made a garland for her head,
>   And bracelets too, and fragrant
>   zone;   [zone-band, belt]
> She looked at me as she did love,
>   And made sweet moan.
>
> "I set her on my pacing steed,
>   And nothing else saw all day long,
> For sideways would she bend, and sing
>   A fairy's song.
>
> "She found me roots of relish sweet,
>   And honey wild, and manna dew;

And sure in language strange she said—
    'I love thee true.'

"She took me to her elfin grot,   [grot-grotto, cave]
    And there she wept and sighed full sore,
And there I shut her wild wild eyes
    With kisses four.

"And there she lullèd me asleep,
    And there I dreamed—Ah!
        woe betide!   [woe betide-alas]
The latest dream I ever dreamed   [latest-last]
    On the cold hill's side.

"I saw pale kings, and princes too,
    Pale warriors, death-pale were they all;
They cried—'La Belle Dame sans Merci
    Hath thee in thrall!'   [thrall-bondage]

"I saw their starved lips in the gloam,   [gloam-twilight]
    With horrid warning gapèd wide,
And I awoke, and found me here
    On the cold hill's side.

"And this is why I sojourn here,
    Alone and palely loitering,
Though the sedge is withered from the lake,
    And no birds sing."

This is Keats' famous "La Belle Dame Sans Merci" (The
Beautiful Lady Without Mercy)—and though it is a passionate poem it is also, I would argue, a poem quite without metaphor. It is almost, in fact, a poem without meaning, a poem of music and mood and infinite magic. This
is great poetry, moving and memorable poetry, but it
communicates subliminally: Keats is not trying to tell us
anything at all, in linear terms. This is not either an allegory, or a bit of realistic description, or—like even
Aesop's fables—a story with a moral, with an articulatable
"point." Keats catches us at once: "alone and palely loitering" is a brilliant invention, in good part because the usual
connotations of "loitering" do not have the mystery and
wonder which are here attached to that word by "alone"
and "palely." And when he follows this kind of inventive-
ness with "The sedge has withered from the lake,/ And

no birds sing," we are more than caught, we are impaled. We do not know, and we have no way of knowing, what lake Keats is talking about. It has no physical location, no name, no existence in any real world. Why has the sedge disappeared? Why, in fact, has it "withered," rather than vanished in some different way? What *meaning* can we attach to the nonpresence of the sedge? The most that can be said, I think, is that the seasons have changed, and with the colder weather the sedge has been destroyed. But this raises almost as many questions as it answers. What do the seasons have to do with the poem's "Knight at arms"? Is the poem supposed to be a kind of parable on the goodness of Spring and the harshness of Winter? Hardly! We can take the inquiry only just so far, and then it stops, because it is meant so to stop. So too with the magnificently cadenced final line of this first stanza, "And no birds sing." Birds do not sing in winter—but in the second stanza it is suggested that the season is autumn, not winter: "The squirrel's granary is full,/ And the harvest's done." There is, quite simply, a perfect finality about "And no birds sing": it summarizes and authenticates the sad barrenness of the "Knight at arm's" wretchedness.

If the poem is not, then, entirely without meaning, what meaning it has must be understood to be suggestive rather than explicit. This is not nonsense poetry: John Keats is not Lewis Carroll. But "La Belle Dame Sans Merci" reaches past our consciousness, down into areas that psychologists and psychiatrists are only beginning to be able to explore. I can give you a good many rationalizations for Keats' success, here, but the final truth is that I do not know. I do not, in the usual sense of the word, "understand" this poem; I feel very sure that no one in the usual sense understands it, or can understand it. I feel equally sure that Keats himself did not "understand" the poem: he released the magic from within himself, but he had no need to be articulate about the nature and sources of that magic. In another sense of the word, however, in the sense in which this poem is a *non*linear experience, Keats of course understands it. He is using the poetic tool of indirection for all it is worth; he is relying on effects he can control, and shape, but the full content of which he cannot articulate, and does not need or want to articulate. Good poetry makes its own context, as I said earlier in this chapter. Keats has located his poem's context in good part below the consciousness line.

And yet "La Belle Dame Sans Merci" is not an obscure poem. It takes a very high art to manage this—Keats is a very great poet—but it *is* possible for poetry to communicate almost nothing on the conscious level and yet still not give us a frustrating sense of trying to communicate on that level, and failing. Keats has given us a seamless structure; we do not have more, we do not want more. Who bothers to wonder just why the "pale kings, and princes too," come crying in the knight-victim's dream? Who cares who La Belle Dame Sans Merci is, or isn't? It does not matter at all. Why are the kings and princes possessed of "starving lips"? It does not matter, and I for one do not wonder.

Nor does it make sense to depreciate this poem's value, on the grounds that it has remarkably little conscious, linear meaning. It is not *Hamlet,* nor was it meant to be: at the level of poetic achievement which "La Belle Dame Sans Merci" reaches, it is frankly silly to make evaluative comparisons. Was Walter Johnson more valuable than Ty Cobb? Is Picasso better than Rembrandt? Mozart or Beethoven, Verdi or Wagner—but why waste one's breath?

The more lyrical (song-like) a poem, the less reliance it *needs* to have on metaphor, or on meaning more generally. Lyric poems can be, and often are, passionately metaphorical, but they can also be like the metaphor-less "La Belle Dame Sans Merci," or the Prologue to William Morris' *The Earthly Paradise,* which begins:

> Of Heaven or Hell I have no power to sing,
> I cannot ease the burden of your fears,
> Or make quick-coming death a little thing,
> Or bring again the pleasure of past years,
> Nor for my words shall ye forget your tears,
> Or hope again for aught that I can say,
> The idle singer of an empty day.
> . . .
> Dreamer of dreams, born out of my due time,
> Why should I strive to set the crooked straight?
> Let it suffice me that my murmuring rhyme
> Beats with light wing against the ivory gate,
> Telling a tale not too importunate
> To those who in the sleepy region stay,
> Lulled by the singer of an empty day.

Morris operates at a much lower level than does Keats, but his disclaimer is remarkably accurate. He is precisely an "idle singer of an empty day," neither more nor less.

This is obviously not true of lyric poetry as a whole: I have tried to make it very clear that while lyric poetry has less intrinsic need of metaphor, it very often makes full use of it. Yeats and Emily Dickinson are two examples of deeply metaphorical lyricists—so much so that even their letters burst into metaphor. Writing in defense of his editorial decisions as an anthologist, for example, Yeats says:

> When I excluded Wilfred Owen, whom I consider unworthy of the poets' corner of a country newspaper, I did not know I was excluding a revered sandwichboard Man of the revolution and that some body has put his worst and most famous poem in a glass-case in the British Museum—however if I had known it I would have excluded him just the same. He is all blood, dirt and sucked sugar stick . . .

How like this is to Yeats' poetry, which similarly bursts into metaphors like "From man's blood-sodden heart are sprung/ Those branches of the night and day/ Where the gaudy moon is hung," or "We that have done and thought,/ That have thought and done,/ Must ramble, and thin out/ Like milk spilt on stone."

Emily Dickinson's letters are so metaphorical that they scarcely seem prose—or even intelligible, sometimes. "I did not deem that planetary forces annulled," she wrote to a friend just become a soldier in the Civil War, "but suffered an exchange of territory, or world. I should have liked to see you before you became improbable. War feels to me an oblique place." The year before, in response to some bewildered criticism of her poems, she had written to the same man: "I thanked you for your justice, but could not drop the bells whose jingling cooled my tramp. Perhaps the balm seemed better, because you bled me first."

> The Spider holds a Silver Ball
> In unperceived Hands—
> And dancing softly to Himself
> His Yarn of Pearl—unwinds—
>
> He plies from Nought to Nought—
> In unsubstantial Trade—

Supplants our Tapestries with His—
In half the period—

An Hour to rear supreme
His Continents of Light—
Then dangle from the Housewife's Broom—
His Boundaries—forgot—

Again, the frame of mind is much the same, expressed
in prose or in verse. To a very considerable extent, metaphor is exactly that: a frame of mind, a way of looking
out at other people's world from an inside world of private
thought and feeling. "War feels to me an oblique place"
expresses the same quality of perception as the poetic
line which has the spider "dangle from the Housewife's
Broom." There is the same sense of distance, the same
curious involvement without commitment: Emily Dickinson is perpetually determined to be herself and only herself,
to present only a single unitary face to the experience of
being alive. So, too, the Yeats who describes Wilfred Owen's
poems as "all blood, dirt and sucked sugar stick," and
who also writes of "those branches of the night and day"
which are sprung "from man's blood-sodden heart." The
vision is the same, the clear, bold awareness of violence
and stunning contrast. Yeats' use of "sucked sugar stick"
has a quite specific relationship to his use of "gaudy moon,"
both metaphors evoking a nauseating sweetness which bitter
once-idealists come to see as only apparent sweetness, not
at all real.

The consistency of psychology should not be surprising.
Is anyone surprised when one painting by Matisse looks
like another painting by Matisse, or when cars built by
General Motors are forever unlike cars built by Volkswagen
or Renault? Poets are people, and poetry is their work.
And metaphor is the canvas they draw on, the metal they
hammer and paint.

Footnote to Chapter Two

It may be that both Tillyard and myself are too much
under the influence of T. S. Eliot's famous essay, "The
Metaphysical Poets" (1921), which argues that while "the
poets of the seventeenth century . . . possessed a mechanism

of sensibility which could devour any kind of experience ... in [this same] seventeenth century a dissociation of sensibility set in, from which we have never recovered." John Donne, says Eliot, experienced "thought as immediately as the odour of a rose." For later poets, he goes on, thought and feeling are separate categories, a disastrous split which has furthered improvements in poetic language without corresponding improvements in delicacy and accuracy of thought and feeling. (Thought + feeling = sensibility.) There is no need to swallow the theory whole —indeed, Eliot did not mean it as a theory, but just as a tool, a speculative perception, useful for explaining certain kinds of historical changes.

But Eliot's distinction does help us to understand why, for example, poets before Donne and Jonson could move easily between poetry of statement and metaphorically more intense poetry, while after their time many poets have to work either one vein or the other. Both kinds of poetry are richly sown through Shakespeare's work, and Sidney's, and Wyatt's, and even Spenser's (though Spenser by temperament leans heavily toward statements and conceits). But George Herbert (1593–1633) is already a follower of Donne, while Robert Herrick (1591–1674), his almost exact contemporary, is distinctly one of the so-called "sons of Ben [Jonson]."

And later periods of English poetry show pretty decided swings between one tendency or the other. John Milton (1608–1674), not just a great poet but, like Shakespeare, a Titan of poetry, briefly unites the two tendencies—but he also indulges himself in so vast and powerful a rhetoric that he overwhelms many smaller fry for more than a century. (Even so fine a poet as Wordsworth, so far distant as the early nineteenth century, was more influenced by Milton than by any other single poetic source.) And Dryden and Pope, the masters of the late seventeenth and early eighteenth centuries, were working in a climate where statement was preferred to intense metaphor. This is of course not just a matter of poetic development: poetry develops out of poets' lives, and life in England and in all of Europe stressed, in Dryden and Pope's lifetimes, the balance and rationality of existence. It was the time of deist philosophy (God as the great clock-maker), of formal gardens, of elaborately contrapuntal music (Handel, Telemann, Bach), of social formality and order.

Eliot's distinction tends to disintegrate, I think, in the nineteenth century, though it is at some points useful.

Byron is certainly more like Pope than he is like Donne, but then again Pope is more like Donne than is usually recognized—and Donne himself also wrote poetry of statement! And the distinction becomes positively silly if applied to poets like Keats and Wordsworth.

CHAPTER THREE: What Poetry Does: Other Tools

I want to explore, in this chapter, a number of basic poetic tools: (1) rhythm and music, (2) contrasts and balance, (3) precision and neatness, (4) control, and (5) obscurity. (Aspects of form and structure will take us into a separate chapter, immediately following this one.)

(1) Rhythm and music

Musicality is poetry's bedrock. A truly unmusical poem is as impossible as unheard music, or invisible sculpture. Some poetic music may be harsh, but that is not the same thing as unmusicality: I do not expect Stravinsky to sound like Mozart, or a gravelly-voiced taxi dispatcher to sound like a trained lyric soprano.

> *The Anglo-Saxon Chronicle: 975 A.D.*
> In this year ended the earthly pleasures
> Of Edgar, King of England, who sought
> A different and lovelier light and left
> This worthless life for one more lasting.
> And all men everywhere on earth, and in England,
> Properly schooled in the science of numbers,
> Know that the King, the young ring-giver,
> Left the world and his life in the month
> Named after Julius, and on its eighth day.
> And after him his half-grown son
> Received the kingdom, and Edward became
> The chief of England's earls, and her King.

> (The translation is my own.)
> K. Feiling, *A History of England*, 1949
> But the peace which only a
> king could keep was destroyed
> when Edgar died, leaving two
> young boys, sons of different
> mothers. Though the elder,
> Edward the Martyr, was

crowned by the archbishops,
his step-mother would not
submit . . .

Apart from differences in historical perspective, and in the type of information conveyed, the chief distinction between the old chronicler and the contemporary historian is that one writes in verse and the other in prose. There is no doubt about either classification: Professor Feiling writes a comfortable, easy prose, and the unknown chronicler moves smoothly along the prescribed stepping stones of Old English verse. The nature of that verse is basically rhythmical. The chronicler uses some literary rhetoric—"a different and lovelier light," "the King, the young ring-giver"—but his verse is largely unadorned. It moves forward with a steady four-beat stress, made more euphonius by frequent alliteration (alliterating consonant with consonant, but also vowel with vowel). This chronicle passage becomes poetry via the subordination of both speech rhythm and prose rhythm —which are unlike each other and are also unlike the rhythm of poetry—to the chronicler's particular pattern of poetic rhythm. That is, the poet's mold is different from the mold of speech, and again different from the mold of prose. People have different oral styles: it would be hard, language apart, to mistake Franklin Delano Roosevelt for Adolf Hitler, or Hitler for Winston Churchill. That prose writers employ different rhythms is I think too obvious to need more than bare statement. Simply call to mind, say, a story by Franz Kafka and a story by William Faulkner, let alone a corporation report or a federal income tax statute.

But it is one thing to be aware that there are differences, and something rather more difficult to be able to understand what those differences are, and especially how they come into being. It is not, first of all, that prose has no rhythm, or even that its rhythms cannot sometimes approximate those of poetry. There would be no prose-poems, if that were true, and poets as different as Baudelaire, Alan Dugan, and T. S. Eliot have made very good use of the prose-poem form. Rather, it is that the rhythm of prose is built, is founded, on syntax. That is, the grammatical organization of an English utterance is the bedrock of English prose—which is a very logical state of affairs, since the chief purpose of prose is and always has been the conveying of information. Literary prose is only a tiny proportion of the prose published every year, and an even smaller proportion of the prose written but not published (letters, memoranda, and the like). Now, syntax is an ideational notion: that is, syntax is fundamentally concerned with the transmission of intellectually oriented material. *Its* rhythms, accordingly, necessarily stress the virtues of clarity and balance, of order, of linear organization. "But the peace which only a king could keep was destroyed when Edgar died, leaving two young boys, sons of different mothers." Poetry doesn't talk that way, doesn't move that way. If a contemporary poet had wanted to say anything of this sort in verse, it might have looked like this:

> Kings can keep peace
> If kings can keep the breath
> In their faces.
> But kings can die.
> And Edgar died,
> And instead of a king
> There were two boys
>   And two mothers.

I doubt that Yeats or Eliot would feel threatened by these freshly concocted lines. The significant thing, here, is how differently this "poem" organizes its rhythm. Instead of standard syntactical patterns being the determiner of word order, and of emphasis, and to some extent of even the choice of words to be used, the poetic version tries—as a contemporary poet would—to stress other elements. It is not as good as the prose version, as a conveyer of information; it is perhaps better as a conveyer of certain emotional states (though this is hardly deeply felt poetry!). And its rhythm is incredibly different.

Another poet, and especially one writing at a different time, would have had yet another rhythm. If Pope, for example, had versified Professor Feiling's prose, his version might have begun like this:

> A king firm on his throne holds peace in his hand,
> A king, dying, lets anarchy loose in his land.

It is not just that Pope would have worked in different verse pattern, but also that he would, again, have needed to stress different things. Kingship meant a great deal more to him than it possibly can to most people alive today—and so on. One of the followers of John Donne might have composed still a different organization, with yet another rhythm:

> Give a king two flowers
> To plant in his land
> And see how mourning showers
> Shake petal and strand.

Again, too, the emphasis would reflect the concerns of the poet's time: matters of succession were vital, in the age of Elizabeth I.

I do not care what name is given to these differences. As I said at the very start of this book, I am less interested in terminology than in substance, less interested in classification than I am in presenting the actual processes by which poetry operates. There has been plain syntactical variation, in each of the three hypothetical poetic versions (all of them of course concocted by me). The twentieth-century version places a syntactically unnecessary stress on the word "king," saying it in all five times over before juxtaposing it against the word "boy." For the hypothetical twentieth-century poet, the fallibility of kings would seem to be the point, and he bends syntax to suit. The make-believe Pope version introduces a kingly throne, and places heavy stress (both ideational and rhythmical) on the virtues of order and authority, and the directly antithetical vices of disorder and anarchy. This too necessarily bends syntax: it would seem that the actual Edgar interests the hypothetical Pope less than the philosophical generalizations suggested by his case. And the pretend-Donne not only stresses kingly succession, but also works out of a context incurably centered around the poetry of love and its lyrical expression. He is not only more elaborately metaphorical, but he cannot resist the slightly awful pun of "mourning showers," or the very dim and obscure pun on "strand"—recall how, in Samuel Johnson's poem "London," the Strand symbolized London itself. None of these versions are worth very much as conveyers of information; none of them even attempt to follow the subject-verb-object word order of usual written English. And yet the rhythms of each are clearly poetic, quite as clearly, I would argue, as the straightforward rhythms of Professor Feiling belong to prose.

It should be clear, too, that musicality is not simply a matter of rhythm. *Everything* verbal has a rhythm of some sort; even quite regular rhythms are not enough, in themselves, to produce musicality. "The king denied the charge, his queen replied, and all the tired men resumed their daily tasks, distinctly bored as well as tired." English is a fundamentally iambic language (see chapter five): in this concocted sentence, stress is followed by unstress, and unstress is followed by stress. To make this perfectly clear, let me indicate the stresses and unstresses, using capital letters and lower-case letters: "the KING deNIED the CHARGE, his QUEEN rePLIED, and ALL the TIred MEN reSUMED their DAIly TASKS, disTINCTly BORED as WELL as TIRED." (If you think I am cheating by making "tired" have two syllables in one place, and only one syllable in another, you have not been reading this aloud.) This is pretty dull stuff, syntactically clear as well as rhythmically patterned, but deeply unmusical. It would fit well in the New York (or the London) *Times:* no sober poet would claim it. Nor is it, again, a simple failure in rhythm which makes this sentence unmusical. Varying the regularity of the rhythm, the alternation of stresses and unstresses, does not improve matters: "The fat king denied the charge, his dumb queen said, and all the tired old men went back to their work, all of them very bored and also tired." Indeed, this ir-regular version is even more clearly unlike poetry: at least, the monotonous regularity of the first version *suggested* something poetic, though the suggestion came to nothing. To turn version one (regular) into version two (irregular), of course, I have had to change words, adding, subtracting, altering. There is nothing improper about that: words are the only building blocks a writer has to work with. And either of these versions can be made musical, note, by exactly this same process of verbal alteration:

(1) The king said no, said no;
    His queen spoke.
    The tired men broke ranks
    And lifted their hoes.

(2) Sweating, the fat slob of a king said
    No,
    No, he hadn't.
    The queen gawked: "No,
    He said. He said no.
    See?"
    The tough old men never blinked,
    Just shuffled down the hill
    And began to dig
    Again.

I have deliberately put these new versions, first in rhymed verse (no/ spoke/ hoes) and then in unrhymed verse, to show—I hope—that the presence or absence of rhyme is not very significant. It is not insignificant: a poor poem can sometimes be helped by excellent rhyming, can be helped musically as well as in other ways. But rhyme is not *necessary*. And I think that both these new versions, whatever their weight as expressions of human feeling, have that indefinable something which makes them musical, which makes them poetry.

This sort of thing is easier for me to do than to analyze, but certain things are fairly plain. Each of these new versions has a *rhetoric,* as well as a rhythm. That is, the *use* of words in each version is consistent, and molded into an emotional and also an ideational pattern. New version number one has a rhetoric which is spare, but also dramatic. The poet seems to speak from a distance, or from a high hill (in classical mythology, poetry descended from, and dead poets ascended to, Mount Olympus). The words have the flavor of an announcement, a pronouncement. There is almost something vatic (prophetic) in the sound of these four lines. But new version number two employs a very different rhetoric, not at all spare, nor restrained, nor distant. The poet is right down in the scene of action: "the fat slob of a king," "the queen gawked." Where the first version is formal, the second is positively slangy: "He said no./ See?" And the social perspective is equally different. Poet number one would not be likely to mount the barricades of a revolution; he would more likely drink cognac than beer. Poet number two is, or at least might be, an activist, and in Italy, say, or France, he might well be (like Louis Aragon, a brilliant poet) a member of the native Communist Party.

And this *rhetoric,* or use of words, works together with, is even in important ways inseparable from, the rhythm of each version. Classical rhetoric seems to suggest restrained rhythm—and version number one, which uses a kind of classical rhetoric, also uses a simple and on the whole regular rhythmic pattern: "the KING said NO, said NO;/ his QUEEN SPOKE./ the TIRed MEN broke RANKS/ and LIFTed their HOES." (This becomes even more regular, if you notice that "queen," though a one-syllable word, is a very long, a very protracted one syllable.) There is no need to diagram out version two: its rhythm, like its rhetoric, is more jagged, more immediate, more the rhythm of this moment than any rhythm belonging to an ancient and more orderly civilization. More poets write in rhythms, and in rhetorics, like those of version number two, these days. That should surprise no one.

This is not the whole story; no book, no teacher, can tell you everything. But some examples from the practice of well-known poets should help to flesh things out. (I choose well-known poets because, simply, you are more likely to have met their work before, and it is easier to see the rhetoric and the rhythm of something familiar.) No poet is better-known than Shakespeare:

> . . . a little Western flower,
> Before milk-white, now purple with love's wound,
> And maidens call it love-in-idleness.
> Fetch me that flower.
>> (*A Midsummer Night's Dream*)

> . . . How is it
> That this lives in thy mind? What seest thou else
> In the dark backward and abysm of time?
>> (*The Tempest*)

A ruler speaks, in each case—but read these lines aloud and note how differently their movement goes. Oberon, ruler of the fairies, speaks the first passage; Prospero, a deposed duke of Milan, speaks the second. The first passage flows, almost skips. The rhetoric is lyrical, and the rhythm matches. The second passage (which dates roughly fifteen years after the first) is altogether more deliberate, more solemn. The last line, in particular, demands a measured, careful speaking: you cannot trip lightly through "in the dark backward and abysm of time." The very sound of the words prevents rapid speaking; the solemn sense requires it equally strongly. Both passages are musical, but Oberon's is the music of fantasy and other-worldly charm, and Prospero's is (in Wordsworth's words) "the still, sad music of humanity." There is no question of better or worse, neither in rhetoric nor in rhythm. A poem is superbly musical when its music is appropriate. In certain Italian operas of the nineteenth century, heroines go mad, or grieve wildly, while the orchestra goes TUM-ti-TUM, TUM-ti-TUM. This is not, to our taste, appropriate, and we prefer Verdi to Bellini, Wagner to Donizetti.

John Milton, like Shakespeare (whom he much resembles, though he hasn't Shakespeare's enormous range), is a master rhetorician—and his use of rhythm is beautifully tuned to match:

This is the Month, and this the happy morn
Wherein the Son of Heaven's eternal King
Of Wedded Maid, and Virgin Mother born,
Our great redemption from above did bring . . .
    ("On the Morning of Christ's Nativity")

Here lies old Hobson, Death hath broke his
    girt,   [girt-belt on a pack horse]
And here, alas, hath laid him in the dirt,
Or else the ways being foul,   [ways-roads]
    twenty to one,
He's here stuck in a
    slough, and overthrown.[slough-impassable muddy place]
'Twas such a shifter, that if truth were known,   ['Twas-
        it was, "it" meaning old Hobson; shifter-cunning fellow]
Death was half glad when he had got him down.
    ("On the University Carrier [coachman, deliveryman]
    who sickened in the time of his vacancy [idleness],
    being forbid to go to London, by reason of the
    Plague")

The elevated rhetoric of the first passage (both passages
were written at roughly the same time, and both are early
Milton) is accompanied by a stately rhythm. If you conjure
up music, for this passage, you hear a stately Handel
melody, slow, easy, full, majestic. The second passage uses
a clearly different vocabulary, and uses it in a tone totally
unlike that of the first passage. It is a deeply appropriate
change, as the subject changes from the sacred to the
entirely profane. Milton liked old Hobson (aged 81, incidentally, when involuntary idleness killed him), but one
does not "like" Jesus in anything like the same sense.
Again, the movement of the second passage is plainer, even
jerkier. The first passage has the sustained sweep appropriate to devotion; the second has the loping gait appropriate,
in Milton's time and in Milton's mind, to a poem about a
lowly carter, an uneducated man of the people.

One more pair of examples, this time from Wordsworth,
another master rhetorician (though slightly less powerful
a master of rhythm):

I heard a thousand blended notes,
While in a grove I sate reclined,
In that sweet mood when pleasant thoughts
Bring sad thoughts to the mind.

    ("Lines Written in Early Spring")

A whirl-blast from behind the hill
Rushed o'er the wood with startling sound;
Then—all at once the air was still,
And showers of hailstones pattered round.
                    ("A Whirl-Blast from behind the Hill")

The first passage begins a sober, philosophical poem. The rhetoric is quietly elevated, the rhythm is easy, distinctly low-keyed. Written in the same year, in the same meter, and with the same rhyme-scheme, the second passage begins a poem of excited celebration, of glorying in the beauty and wonder of Nature. The rhythm whips up the excitement, galloping straight up to the full, and dramatic, stop of "Then—." The pause echoes the pause observed in Nature, and very deliberately so. And when the rhythm picks up, after the pause, it has changed, become quieter, slower. The rhetoric too becomes muted: instead of *blasts rushing* "with startling sound," we have "still" air and hailstones *pattering*.

Like metaphor, then, musicality is both a tool and an intrinsic part of the substance of a poem. Any separation is for purposes of analysis and commentary: no real separation into "style" versus "substance," or "rhetoric" versus "meaning," or any similar pairing, is in the end meaningful. What makes this even plainer is the fact that a fine poet, like a fine singer, has a distinctive "voice." Milton can sound like Shakespeare, and Wordsworth can sound like Milton, but mostly each sounds only like himself, each is distinctive and inimitable. Which also makes perfectly good sense: if a poet is, as I insist, only a man who expresses himself in poetry, rather than in the building of bridges or the making of matches, to the extent that he truly does express *himself* he will be uniquely whatever he happens to be. To the extent that he lacks the force of personality necessary to have a distinctive self, so too will his poetic voice blur and go fuzzy. To the extent that he is content to imitate someone else's voice, instead of struggling for his own—and it is always a struggle, and protracted, and terribly hard—he will similarly seem less clear, less anything very much in particular. And to the extent that he is content to parade false feelings, false ideas, in his poetry, he will seem neither memorable nor even interesting. Who wants to stand still and be bombarded by lie after lie, by cliché after cliché? If it is no harder to be a great poet than a great architect or a great physicist, it is also no easier.

(2) *Contrasts and balance*

I've talked about metaphor as a process of association, a process of discovering similarities between things not obviously alike. It would have been more accurate, really, to talk about a process of association *and dissociation*, a discovering of both similarities and dissimilarities. Some poets prefer one of these two ways of looking at things: John Donne, for example, is particularly fond of dissociations:

> Busy old fool, unruly Sun,
> Why dost thou thus
> Through windows, and through curtains, call on us?

Our whole sense of time, daily and yearly, moves as the sun moves: it is the very symbol of regularity and order, of motion according to *rule*. But with a neat pun, Donne turns reality upside down, making the sun *un*ruly ("disorderly"). "Busy" is a pun, too—it means someone who works hard and regularly, but also someone who is meddlesome, officious, prying—and the meaning which Donne concentrates on is shown by the next two words, "old fool." You are not pleased to be visited by an "old fool." And again, this is dissociative, for what (especially in cold, damp England) is more welcome than the warm sun? Yet Donne tells us that the sun is a meddling, disorderly peeping tom—and the dissociation is not simply arbitrary or wilful. *Most* people may like the dawn, and welcome the light, but a lover locked in his belovèd's arms does not. The sun, and the world with it, may rejoice at rising, but the lover resents having to break away. And the dissociation, which shocks and shakes us, compels us to be attentive to Donne's purpose. He forces us to listen—and he also pleases us, by demonstrating that his dissociative metaphor has a clear and sensible reason for shocking and shaking us.

Alexander Pope, in many ways a very different poet, often does exactly this same thing. Describing Belinda's toilet table, in *The Rape of the Lock*, he writes:

> Here Files of Pins extend their shining Rows,
> Puffs, Powders, Patches, Bibles, Billet-doux.

The list of objects runs from pins, puffs, powders, patches (black patches pasted on a woman's cheeks, to look like "beauty-marks" or moles), straight through to a gross dissociation, *Bibles*. This is dissimilarity enough, but Pope runs smoothly past, to *Billet-doux*, as though the negative element, the dissociation were not there—which heightens the mocking effect. It's even cleverer than that, since the first line of this couplet uses a subtly positive association to strengthen the image. Soldiers in rows are in military language often called "files" of soldiers; with their weapons and armor gleaming, they too stand in "shining Rows." This quietly prepares us to expect further similarities and strengthenings, and the second line seems to be giving them to us, only to slide, suddenly, into the dissociation of *Bibles*. (Pope is full of complex and delicate things like this—which is one reason why it takes time for beginning readers of poetry to feel entirely comfortable with him.)

There are hundreds of ways of using dissociations. John Skelton's "Colin Clout," written in 1522, begins:

> What can it avail
> To drive forth a snail,
> Or to make a sail
> Of an herring's tail?

These opening lines are preceded by an epigraph, in Latin, which in English translation reads, "Who will rise up with me against evil-doers? or who will stand up with me against the workers of iniquity? No one, O Lord!" (The passage is from Psalm 94, Vulgate version.) Skelton's clear purpose is to attack both evil-doers and the futility of trying to do good: even if I make a sail out of a herring's tail, which takes a lot of doing, what will I have accomplished? The dissociation sets the tone, and off he runs: it's a rollicking poem.

Tennyson does it, too, though at greater length:

> Ah God! the petty fools of rhyme
> That shriek and sweat in pygmy wars
> Before the stony face of Time,
> And looked at by the silent stars . . .

The contrast, here, is between the immensity of Time and of the stars (who, please note, have the sense to be silent), and the immense insignificance of petty poets, squabbling in rhyme, who are explicitly compared to pygmies. This is not as subtle as Pope's usage, nor I think is Tennyson as good a poet as Pope. The significant thing is that the Victorians practiced dissociation almost as much, in their different ways, as did the eighteenth-century poets. When Matthew Arnold speaks, in "Urania," of how "her lovely eyes maintain/ Their pure, unwavering, deep disdain," the tone of every word except the last one is positive. "Disdain" may not toll like a bell, here (Arnold is not that good a poet), but it has much greater force for having been prepared for by a long sequence of its opposites. Even Swinburne, that passionate addict of narcotic nonsense, can write "Her bosom is an oven of myrrh, to bake/ Love's white warm shewbread to a browner cake." (The poem is called "Sonnet for a Picture." *Shewbread*-a sacerdotal bread, a kind of priestly offering used in ancient Israel.) To stretch a point, we can perhaps see an "oven" in a woman's breasts—but "an oven of myrrh" is as surely a dissociation as any image ever put on paper.

Nor, of course, are dissociations limited to English poetry. To take only a single example, James J. Y. Liu, in his superb *The Art of Chinese Poetry* (1962), notes that in one romantic poem a lover "describes his lady as 'soft jade and warm perfume,'" and in the same poem another "lady is described as having 'ice flesh and jade bones.'"

Balance is a slightly queer notion, often best understood (and least well explained) by poets. Many literary critics, and too many teachers of literature, tend to think of balance in structural terms—rather like cooks: so much salt, so much pepper, so much vinegar, so much honey. It all gets measured out, but mostly as if the poet, too, had been a cook, anxious to be sure that his poem followed the proper recipe. Subject matter—ideas, narrative—tends to be stressed, in this kind of analysis, rather than the living process of the poetry. If Milton gives an inning to God, these critics are apt to point out, he nevertheless preserves balance by giving the next inning to the Devil. This kind of balance does of course exist; it is important. It is not however as important as is often thought, nor is it as difficult to talk about as the kind of balance I want to comment on.

Since Shakespeare is, in my view, the best-balanced poet in the world, in any language, let me start with him. His *King Henry the Fifth* begins with a speech by way of prologue:

> O for a Muse of fire, that would ascend
> The brightest heaven of invention,
> A kingdom for a stage, princes to act,
> And monarchs to behold the swelling scene!
> Then should the warlike Henry, like himself . . .

All the elements of balance are present: continuity, logic, moderation. (Classicists may understand my use of "balance" better, indeed, if I say that *mensura* is really what I have in mind. Here, as almost always, Shakespeare fairly reeks of it.) The sun god, Apollo, who dwells in "the brightest heaven," is also the god of poetry. He is thus doubly a "Muse of fire" here, since "fire" in fact "ascends" as it burns. Shakespeare has tightly joined the two kinds of heat, physical and literary. And this celestial "invention" alone, he tells us, would permit him to properly narrate King Henry the Fifth's story. Without the help of heaven, thus actively intervening, the poet, says the prologue, is in trouble. With such intervention, the poet would not be limited to a grubby little stage, in a grubby earth-bound playhouse. He would have a "kingdom" for his stage, and his players would not be actors, ordinary men (today aping a prince, tomorrow aping a clown), but actual princes, with kings as the audience. ("The swelling scene" is a typical Elizabethan playwright's phrase—echoed by T. S. Eliot in his "The Love Song of J. Alfred Prufrock"—and meaning only "filling out, growing in intensity.") *Then,* says the prologue, then, given these preconditions, "warlike Henry" could be seen "like himself." Without these fabulous aids, however, the earth-bound scene, the earth-bound players, and the earth-bound playwright, will have to do what they can, knowing quite well that they cannot show King Henry the Fifth "like himself."

These opening five lines of the play are all dovetailed, like intricate mother-of-pearl, though the seams do not show and to the casual eye nothing remarkable may have been accomplished. (The effect of the highest art, in all art forms, is frequently the concealing of art—making something complex and extremely difficult seem simple and straightforward, clear as a bell.) The dovetailing is fully consecutive; the continuity, in short, is perfect, never dropped, never flagging. All the metaphors are interrelated; all are ideally chosen for the poet's purpose. The poetic logic, too, is thus flawless. And so sure is Shakespeare's touch, so balanced, that he does not linger at any point along the way. Each new idea is presented when we are ready for it, and each idea, once presented, is the stepping stone to the next idea. Nothing is flogged to death, there is no sense of strain, no aura of immoderation.

How rare and difficult this in fact is, though as I say it does not seem at all difficult, can, I suspect, best be seen if we look at some inferior examples. Virtually everyone is inferior to Shakespeare. I do not mean to set up strawmen, however: these will be inferior examples, but chosen from the work of recognized poetic craftsmen, competent poets who do not have anything like Shakespeare's supreme capacity, his almost unerring balance. Edwin Markham was once famous for his 1899 poem, "The Man with the Hoe." It begins:

> Bowed by the weight of centuries he leans
> Upon his hoe and gazes on the ground,
> The emptiness of ages in his face,
> And on his back the burden of the world.
> Who made him dead to rapture and despair,
> A thing that grieves not and that never hopes,
> Stolid and stunned, a brother to the ox?

"The emptiness of ages" bothers me exceedingly—but there is no need to discuss Markham's rhetoric, here. There is continuity, in this passage, but it is stretched: the poet leans too hard on each point along the way, and we are likely to grow either impatient or bored. If, for example, the man with the hoe (the agricultural worker, and by secondary extension the laboring classes more generally) is bowed, leaning on his hoe, and staring at the ground—as Markham very clearly tells us he is—we know that he is not likely to be considering the habits of ants and grass-hoppers, or solving problems in spherical trigonometry. The picture is plainly of someone dulled and oppressed ("bowed by the weight of centuries"), blankened. Yet Markham goes on to tell us about that "emptiness of ages in his face" —and even then he is not done explaining the man's state to us. Having already drawn the portrait overly full, he now adds to "the weight of centuries" (which is after all a fairly heavy notion) "the burden of the world." But how much can "the burden of the world" add, in fact, that is not already contained in the earlier image? Fine: we know, by now abundantly clearly, that the man with the hoe is beaten down, unable to feel—or at least so the innocent reader might think. Markham apparently thought other-wise, for he goes on to assure us that his pitiful hero is "dead to rapture and despair," and then, still unsure that we have gotten the point, tells us in the next line that this crushed-out human creature "grieves not" and "never hopes," all of which adds nothing we did not know—but to which is then added "stolid and stunned," which I am afraid rather gilds the lily. To be sure, poetic tastes change, and have changed since Markham's time. The kind of overblown, immoderate rhetoric he indulges in was far more acceptable in 1899 than it can be today. It may well be that some future swing in taste will make Markham

seem less disastrously ineffective, in this passage, than I
have made him out to be. But no swing in taste, I am con-
vinced, can go far enough to make Markham's lines seem
as balanced as Shakespeare's.

Not all late nineteenth-century rhetoric is deficient in
balance, however deficient it may seem to us in other re-
spects. In "My Sister's Sleep," as sentimental and unat-
tractive as a poem by a good poet can be, Dante Gabriel
Rossetti writes:

> Her little work-table was spread
> With work to finish. For the glare
> Made by her candle, she had care
> To work some distance from the bed.

This is third-rate poetry, but not because its balance is poor.
Indeed, the balance is extremely good; continuity, logic,
and moderation are unexceptionable, here. Rossetti is the
better craftsman—in spite of which I would myself prefer,
given the choice, to read Markham. Craft by itself is simply
not enough.

> So shoots a star as doth my mistress glide
> At midnight through my chamber, which she makes
> Bright as the sky when moon and stars are spied,
> Wherewith my sleeping eyes amazèd wake . . .

These are the first four lines of a sonnet by John Davies
of Hereford, the Elizabethan poet discussed—and for this
very same sonnet—on the first page of chapter one of this
book. I quoted only one and six-tenths lines, there, and
praised them. But you can now see that, at even the modest
additional length here offered you, Davies of Hereford is
simply not Shakespeare's equal, though he is his contemporary. A shooting star is bright: every fool knows
that. Midnight is dark: this is equally plain. If at midnight
a shooting star comes through a room, what else will it
make that room but "bright"? But Davies of Hereford
pads out the image (perhaps to get "spied" at the end of
the line, in order to have a rhyme for "glide"?), telling us
that his mistress/shooting star turns his room "Bright as
the sky when moon and stars are spied." Having had the
shooting star, did we need that "sky"? And having had
both shooting star and sky, did we then need the "moon
and stars"? We surely did not need *both* moon *and* stars.
Nor, I think, did we need to be told that these luminaries
are "spied" in the sky. I am unfortunately amused at the
solemnity of the poet, in line 4, blandly informing us

that, under the circumstances, his "sleeping eyes" were "amazèd," and he woke up. (Ralph Waldo Emerson, told that Margaret Fuller "accepted the universe," said at once, "She'd damn well better!") With such a blazing Roman Carnival next to his bed, it's lucky for him that he didn't wake screaming in fright, or perhaps on fire. Continuity virtually slows to a standstill, here; logic is not of high importance to the poet; and moderation is quite beyond him. In a word, he is drastically deficient in balance.

(3) *Precision and neatness*

Precision and *neatness* have nothing to do with hand-writing; they are not unrelated to some of the issues just discussed. Precision is a word-by-word matter, depending on the poet's determination never to settle for the second- (or third-) best word, when in time, and with enough sweat, he can find the one right word, *le mot juste*. (The phrase comes naturally in French. A well-read lady once told me that she preferred English poetry to French, since it was warmer and grander and altogether more satisfying, but that she always read philosophy, and especially Oriental philosophy, in French rather than English translations. The French, she said, was so much more naturally logical and clear, precise to the very bone.) I do not mean, here, the kind of inspired brilliance which leads Marvell, in his "The Garden," to speak of "Annihilating all that's made/ To a green Thought in a green Shade." That kind of magic can-not be prescribed, but only worshipped. I mean, rather, the kind of word-by-word accuracy demonstrated, often, in Milton's *Paradise Lost*. In Book I, for example, the Phi-listine god Dagon "mourned in earnest, when the Captive Ark/ Maimed his brute image, head and hands lopped off/ In his own Temple." One principal reason for the strength of both this passage and of the entire poem, is the steady, unrelaxed precision of Milton's language. Telling the story of the Ark of the Covenant, held captive in a pagan temple and taking its revenge on the temple god, Milton marches his words into battle like Roman soldiers. The idol was not "ruined," or "destroyed," or "attacked," or "soiled"; it was —*le mot juste* in action—"maimed." The idol was not simply, and loosely, "pagan," or "savage," or what-have-you, but a "brute image." The precise word cuts out sloppy misunderstanding; it also raises exactly the right echoes. "Brute" carries something of the force of "animal-like," something of the force of "brutal," something of the force of "sheer-strength-but-without-much-brain." Milton could have spun out the story; he could have talked about Dagon being cut to pieces in front of his own altar, in front of his own priests, in the country of his greatest strength, and so on, but he says, with perfect precision, only "In his own Temple"—and the crisp accuracy says it all.

Mary Barnard's exquisite translations of Sappho, the best translations of Sappho the English language has ever been offered, have a different kind of precision. Sappho (and also her translator) is a woman, with concerns and with an approach sharply unlike Milton's.

> If you are squeamish
>
> Don't prod the
> beach rubble

This is all that remains of a longer poem. Most of Sappho's poetry has survived, over the twenty-five hundred years since she wrote, in fragments, bits and snippets. But Miss Barnard makes this fragment complete for us. And her delicate—but not fragile: all delicacy is not fragile!—precision carries much of the load. The key word, I think, is "prod": the Greek fragment is a bare three words, translated by Professor Edmonds, in his *Lyra Graeca* (*Greek Lyrics*), as "stir not the jetsam." But "stir" will not do. This is not a vegetable soup, or a pan of scrambled eggs, which the poet is confronting, but a heap of tangled refuse on the shore. You cannot at once see what is in it; if you are curious, you need to examine it more closely—and yet, not too closely. So you don't lift it up, or pull it apart, or kick it. You take a stick, or use the tip of your shoe, and rather gingerly, but yet with a certain determination, you "prod" it. And just as it does with Milton, the exact right word produces echoes which help the poem to make its effect. Someone or something which does not do what it is supposed to, whether from laziness or some worse motive, requires prodding. Someone who is afraid, but who needs to do something, requires prodding. The primary meaning, of course, remains "to poke about." But art often depends on just these "extras," these additional, bonus effects. The inferior artist cannot achieve them—which is not to say that the superior artist finds them lying on his plate, when he wakes up in the morning. Thomas Edison's definition of the way an inventor works—"one percent inspiration, ninety-nine percent perspiration"—will do for poetry, too.

Neatness is, in my terms, a somewhat larger matter than precision. Alexander Pope is a logical exemplar:

> Now wits gain praise by copying other wits
> As one Hog lives on what another shits.

This delightfully nasty epigram can be praised for all sorts of things, not least the daring and wonderfully successfully repetition of "wits," in line one. It hammers the rhyme word unforgettably home. But the whole point of the little poem lies in its basic image, the filth-loving, belly-mad pig eating the excrement of other pigs, and the neat comparison of pig and plagiarist/would-be wit. This is neat not simply because it is accurate (precise), though it is that too, but because it is perfectly appropriate. There is nothing inevitable about the comparison. Pope himself has six "Couplets on Wit," scribbled in odd moments while he was translating Homer and printed straight down the page, in his collected poems. Each of these "couplets" has a different root image; none of the others is as good as the one I have quoted. It is not inevitability which makes this epigram neatness incarnate, but rightness, the joining of exact language and exact idea, to exactly describe a situation (or a person, a place, a mood—whatever).

Neatness need not be nasty. Robert Herrick (who could be savagely nasty), a contemporary and a follower of Ben Jonson, begins his short poem, "Upon Julia's Clothes":

> When as in silks my Julia goes,
> Then, then (me thinks) how sweetly flows
> That liquefaction of her clothes!

"Silks," "flows," "liquefaction": the basic sequence is perfectly balanced, but again it is something more. The liquid sound of rustling silk is made into a devastatingly erotic comparison. Herrick has found a core image of immensely felicitous sensuality: the motion of the smooth cloth blends inextricably into the smooth motion of the woman wearing the cloth. The lines are of course equally *precise;* the core image also has continuity, logic, and moderation, keeping it in superb *balance*. There are carefully handled technical devices, like the deliberateness of "Then, then," in line two, followed at once by the further postponement enforced by the parenthetical "me thinks." The A-A-A rhyme scheme—goes/ flows/ clothes—enhances *musicality*, and the gently contrastive flowing-river/ flowing-clothing notion also contributes to the overall effectiveness of the passage. It is impossible to be dogmatic and assert that any one of these elements is more important than all the others. Clearly, however, the inherently beautiful *neatness* of the core image is a major factor.

The principle can be observed all up and down the course of English (and of course of non-English) poetry. Speaking of Prometheus, chained to a rock and horribly punished for his defiance of Jove, Shelley writes, in his *Prometheus Unbound:*

> Past ages crowd on thee, but each one remembers,
> And the future is dark, and the present is spread
> Like a pillow of thorns for thy slumberless head.

It is not an intrinsically remarkable image; in context, however, it is singularly apt. The reader experiences a sense of satisfaction, finding the "pillow of thorns" image (with its Christ echoes) used for Prometheus—and the reader's satisfaction is at the heart of all poetry, and of all art. These lines give a sense of something like coming into an unknown room, expecting to find it at best unfamiliar, at worst disorderly, and somehow finding it all very much in place, very tidy, very *neat*.

> Let the crocus air invoke spring.
> Gardens are not impossible.
> Sun steams on the roofs where
> Snow has hung.

This is the first quatrain of "Crocus Air," by the too-little-known American poet, Winfield Townley Scott. Again, there are a lot of ways in which these four lines can be praised, but one chief way is for their fluent rightness, the ease and naturalness with which the clear and right things are said. Whether crocuses invoke spring, or spring invokes crocuses, the association is elemental. Scott does not say: "It has been a long hard winter. I cannot believe in spring. Or gardens." He does not even say, in fact, that he has actually seen a crocus, breaking up through the snow. All he says is that "the crocus air"—the air which seems to smell of crocuses, and therefore of spring—reminds him that spring is possible, gardens are possible, green and growing and warm things are possible. Why, on the frozen city roofs, where instead of flowers and ivy "snow has hung," now, see, "sun steams." The impotent winter sun neither steams nor warms; this seems to be the spring sun, and there is hope. What this quatrain seems to me to have, more than anything else, is that clear, strong cohesiveness which I have called neatness.

> They flee from me that sometime did me seek
>   With naked foot stalking in my chamber.
> I have seen them gentle, tame, and meek
>   That now are wild and do not remember
>   That sometime they put themselves in danger
> To take bread at my hand; and now they range
> Busily seeking with a continual change.

One of the greatest of early sixteenth-century lyrics, this untitled poem by Sir Thomas Wyatt—I have quoted only the first stanza—is a brilliant fusion of images drawn from the world of animals and images of love. It is not the naturalness, here, which charms, but the tightrope walking with which the poet brings us through; the center of the poem seems to move first this way, then that, finally culminating, in this first stanza, with the clearest of sexual criticisms, the charge that his former mistresses "now . . . range/ Busily seeking with a continual change." There is I think nothing inevitable about this particular crossing of images, perhaps because few poets, and especially poets of Wyatt's time, have handled sexual politics with this blunt freedom. (There are some brilliantly unique things about this poem, which I urge you to read in its entirety.) Wyatt ties it all up, ties it all together, in good part because of the force of his indignation, his distinctly moral outrage, but also because each line, though it tends to startle us at first sight, then begins to enchant us with its perfect appropriateness. "Stalking" in his bedroom, "with naked foot": how much neater an image can you have, for nocturnal trysts, for the concealed and risky meetings of lover and mistress. (One of Wyatt's mistresses, before her marriage, had been Anne Boleyn: the blending of sex and politics is not, in short, in any way an accident!) The woman-as-deer comparison comes neatly to the surface with "to take bread at my hand," but it has been at least implicit in adjectives like "gentle, tame, and meek." And the movement from fleeing and stalking *him*, to "seeking" others, promiscuously ("with a continual change"), contains both sexual and hunting images, powerfully blended. The tame deer goes wild, and goes ranging far; the woman won to a taste of sexual freedom, quickly wants more. (I am not speaking morally, here, though Wyatt is.) As always, it is difficult to confine analysis to only one of the aspects which make the stanza memorable: it is memorable for many many reasons. I can myself still remember very clearly the first time I ever read it, more than twenty years ago. I have read it perhaps fifty times over, since then, never for classroom purposes, but strictly for my own excitement. (Simple "pleasure" would be too tame a term, for the experience of this poem.)

> Who says that fictions only and false hair
> Become a verse? Is there in truth no beauty?
> Is all good structure in a winding stair?
> May no lines pass, except they do their duty
>   Not to a true, but a painted chair?

This is the opening of "Jordan," by George Herbert, in some ways the "neatest" of all poets writing in English. Herbert's sense for the appropriate is so continuous, indeed, that it becomes a kind of structural principle in his poetry. —But that begins to take us into the next section of this chapter, on *control*. Note, here, how dense and obscure this stanza seems, on first reading. Then consider the following:

"fictions" = inventions, artificial creations
"false hair" = wigs, representative of female artificiality
"become" = to be appropriate for
"Is there in truth no beauty" = Is there no beauty in truth
"structure" = both architectural and poetic structure
"a winding stair" = literally, the elaborate winding stair structure of aristocratic mansions of the time; representative of the highly elaborate, the ornate, expensive, and complicated *things* of so-called "civilized" and "cultured" existence
"line" = as in architecture or painting (or poetry); the reference may well be to Plato's *Republic*, Book 10, where a distinction is drawn as between a "real" ("true") chair and one concocted by a painter; there are, says Plato, users and makers of objects like chairs, and then there are mere imitators who do not know their "proper quality."
"pass" = pass muster, prove acceptable
"painted chair" = artificially colored, as opposed to "true" or naturally colored

Some of the reader's initial problem, clearly, is a function of the time which has elapsed (some three hundred fifty years) since Herbert wrote. Some of it, too, stems from Herbert's teasingly allusive style. As a follower of John Donne, he is especially fond of saying things allusively rather than saying them directly, and he is deeply attracted to puns, *double-entendres,* and other sorts of wordplay. These initial obstacles overcome—and this is a poem I *have* regularly used in introductory literature courses—the stanza becomes an extremely simple plea for simplicity and naturalness in poetry, as opposed to artificial, "arty" conventions. It is a challenge, delivered in the face of those who maintain the opposite position—those who argue that poetry is a "civilized" and "cultured" art, devoted only to "high" things, things of an elaborate and complicated sort. And these others are, in Herbert's eyes, the majority; he is very much in the minority, he indicates by his strenuous, combative tone. The stanza is *neat,* finally, because of the carefully organized, compressed appropriateness of all the materials handled. Herbert is one hundred per cent relevant, whether you agree with him or not (and surely the complexity of his argument for simplicity is counter productive!). *Relevancy,* indeed, is a perfectly good substitute word for *neatness.*

(4) *Control*

Poetic *control* is, next to musicality, perhaps the most basic and important characteristic of all great verse. It implies, really, an ability to handle *all* the elements of poetic composition—all the things I have been discussing, to this point, and structural complexities as well. (Structure and form will be discussed in chapter four.) The word *control* does not imply manipulation, nor is it used primarily in the sense of governance, of dominance. What *control* suggests is a kind of easy synthesis—and by "easy" I mean unobtrusive, not simple-to-achieve! A poet who has superb control has, then, everything he needs to write great poetry—except, of course, that he must be someone who has felt and thought and experienced enough so that he has something worth saying, with all his expertise. This last requirement is not one that analysis can say very much about. It's a bit like absolute pitch, you either have it or you don't. If you have it, hurrah. If you don't, too bad.

> I think I grow tensions
> like flowers
> in a wood where
> nobody goes.
>
> Each wound is perfect,
> encloses itself in a tiny

imperceptible blossom,
making pain.

Pain is a flower like that one,
like this one,
like that one,
like this one.

This is "The Flower," from Robert Creeley's *For Love*.
One of the very best poets now writing, Creeley has
evolved a technique of singularly high compression; every
word is positioned for maximum leverage. Yet the domi-
nant tone, from a technical point of view, is the clear sense
of sure-footedness, of mastery—or, in a word, of *control*.
The bare, plain language, as "unpoetic" in the traditional
sugary sense as it can be, is nevertheless continuously
evocative. Part of this is Creeley's blatantly honest tenta-
tiveness: this is not a technique or a pose, but the expression of a deeply felt view of things. The reader is kept as
unsure as the poet: is this it? is that it? what is it? where?
Another part of his evocativeness is his inversion of traditional motifs: flowers become "tensions," here, and the
safe security of the wood is turned into "a wood where/
nobody goes." Each flower is then exposed as "each
wound" with its own "tiny/imperceptible blossom," producing no beauty, but "making pain." And the ancient rite
of petal-counting—he loves me, he loves me not, and all
that—is transmuted in the final stanza, delicately and yet
powerfully, into a kind of counting of wounds, rather than
blossoms, a marshalling of pain rather than beauty. The
lines sing, because Creeley has a fine ear, and an ear trained
to the particular kind of music he wants to make: this is
fully personal; Creeley is one of those rare poets who has
a distinctive voice, completely and, by now, effortlessly his
own. As I've said, the metaphors are continually absorb-
ing. The contrasts between traditional and contemporary
stances are carefully worked through. The poem is wonderfully in balance, moving at the exactly right pace from
part to part, moving with seamless, unflawed logic. Precision is of course a chief feature of Creeley's taut style,
and the rightness, or neatness (or relevance) of his poetic
scheme is of a very high order. What results, accordingly,
is a fine poem with superb *control*.

Control is, indeed, a kind of superior diagnostic tool. A
poem which has, or at least on first reading seems to have
it, is worth closer attention; a poem which lacks, or seems
to lack it, is usually not worth the same degree of atten-

tion. (Poems, like music, like painting, are often not fully
digestible on one exposure. But this is the general subject
of obscurity, to which we will turn in a moment.) Weldon
Kees, for example, though a very good poet, is not of
Creeley's stature. Compare Creeley's "The Flower," just
discussed, with Kees' "Land's End":

> A day all blue and white, and we
> Came out of woods to sand
> And snow-capped waves. The sea
> Rose with us as we walked, the land
> Built dunes, a lighthouse, and a sky of gulls.
>
> Here where I built my life ten years ago,
> The day breaks gray and cold;
> And brown surf, muddying the shore,
> Deposits fish-heads, sewage, rusted tin.
> Children and men break bottles on the stones.
> Beyond the lighthouse, black against the sky,
> Two gulls are circling where the woods begin.

This is very competent, in many details; above all, it has
musicality. It has a good deal of precision, too. But the
balance is poor: there is too much of the same sort of
thing, for too long at a time. Nor does the accumulation of
detail seem to go anywhere, to add up to anything very
particular: the poem lacks what I have called neatness (or
relevancy). There are some effective contrasts ("snow-
capped waves," "a sky of gulls"), but nothing seems to
govern them, to unite them in any higher purpose than a
good descriptive image. Description is not enough. One
can say that this poem has not been worked over enough,
that the stuff of reality has not been sufficiently transformed
into the stuff of poetry. One can also say that Kees here
lacks control of his subject matter—does not, perhaps,
quite know what his subject matter is. Creeley is not always so clearly Kees' superior, but he is generally a better
poet, more finished, more in control.

Walt Whitman, though he is capable of extended passages with superb, tight control, and sometimes can manage to control whole poems, is often the very exemplar of
the poet with uncertain control. In his last (1892) edition
of *Leaves of Grass*, there are poems like "To the Leaven'd
Soil they Trod," followed by poems like "When Lilacs
Last in the Dooryard Bloom'd." The first of these begins:

To the leaven'd soil they trod calling I sing for the last,
(Forth from my tent emerging for good, loosing, un-
    tying the tent-ropes),
In the freshness the forenoon air, in the far-stretching
    circuits and vistas again to peace restored,
To the fiery fields emanative and the endless vistas
    beyond . . .

This rather flatulent rhetoric is followed by some of the
greatest elegaic verse ever written:

When lilacs last in the dooryard bloom'd,
And the great star early droop'd in the western sky
    in the night,
I mourn'd, and yet shall mourn with ever-returning
    spring.

Whitman's control wavers, often, within a single poem. In
his long and powerful "Song of Myself," for example, one
minute he can be writing brilliantly.

A child said, *What is the grass?* fetching it to me with
    full hands,
How could I answer the child? I do not know what it
    is any more than he.
I guess it must be the flag of my disposition, out of
    hopeful green stuff woven.—

And the next minute he can be off on a long laundry-list
of no great relevance:

The blab of the pave, tires of carts, stuff of bootsoles,
    talk of the promenaders . . .

In a poet as great as Whitman, it is easy to forgive this
sort of weakness, and read on. With a poet of very doubtful
stature, like Matthew Arnold, the lack of control is virtually
fatal to listener attention:

That son of Italy who tried to blow,
Ere Dante came, the trump of sacred song,
In his light youth amid a festal throng
Sate with his bride to see a public show.

Fair was the bride, and on her front   [front-face]
    did glow
Youth like a star; and what to youth belong—
Gay raiment, sparkling gauds,   [gauds-ornaments]
    elation strong.
A prop gave way! crash fell a platform! lo . . .

Not many of us will last this long. This is positively embarrassing, in places. A poet needs to have infinitely higher standards than this, needs to be infinitely more self-critical. The Russian poet, Innokenty Annensky, once asked about a younger poet, Andrey Biely, who was publishing volume after volume at a fearful rate, "Good God! When does he find time to burn the stuff?" A poet burns quite a lot, if he is aware of the problems of control. Matthew Arnold had almost no sense of control; he pays for it, today, by being in large part both unreadable and unread.

(5) *Obscurity*

Obscurity is something of a red herring. The average person has a deep, stubborn conviction that poetry is inherently obscure (as well as exotic, irrelevant, and perverse). "Tyger! Tyger! burning bright/ In the forests of the night," can be accepted, even admired, because it has the large sound of *P*oetry. That is, the feeling goes, there is neither need to inquire, nor any possibility of learning, what tiger is referred to, or why it is burning bright (maybe because tigers have big eyes?), or why the forests are there (tigers live in *jungles:* we all know that), or in short what the devil the thing is all about. It is *P*oetry—and everyone knows that that means it is "fancy" language, "high" language, "a tale . . . full of sound and fury,/ Signifying nothing." There are, of course, certain experts (of doubtful expertise: a *real* expert, in this view, is a man who can take an automobile apart with his fingernail clipper, or weld steel girders with a cigarette lighter) who claim to understand poetry. Some of them make their living—usually as that anomalous creature, a "professor"— by foisting this asserted, but untestable, "understanding" on the innocent and suffering young. The student is not deceived by the pretense—he knows that *P*oetry means nothing, and that it is not to be taken seriously—but he goes along with the make-believe, for just as long as the academic situation makes it necessary that he do so. The professor gets his salary, the student gets his degree (and the job that follows it, as night follows day), and everybody is happy.

There are "pretend" poets, too—lots of them, many very widely published. (There is Rod McKuen, for example.) The pages of many small and exceedingly bad magazines are full of flatulent mouthings by people who are sure that windy noise—the louder and the windier the better, in this view—is really what poetry is all about. But William

Blake's "tyger" is not windy noise. Blake's England—
really, Blake's London, for he knew the great city more
than he did the countryside—was suffering from the earliest
ravages of the Industrial Revolution. People were out of
jobs, were forced into beggary, were forced into jobs they
neither understood nor enjoyed. Children were started on
lives—brief lives—of servitude and misery. Science was the
great God, and the Church bowed to it, complacently ac-
cepting Reason and forgetting Pity—or Charity. When
Blake thought of the tiger, therefore, he thought of a creature with natural power and grace, with strength and force
and vitality undiminished—and undiminishable—by "mere"
Reason, the pale rationality of that blight on the face of
the natural world, Man. "Is this a holy thing to see," he
asks in "Holy Thursday," another poem in *Songs of Experience*, "In a rich and fruitful land,/ Babes reduced to
misery,/ Fed with cold and usurous hand?" Or as he asks
in "On Another's Sorrow," "Can I see another's woe,/ And
not be in sorrow too?" Blake wanted the tiger and the rose
and the sun-flower to bloom and blossom and live; instead
of "tomb-stones where flowers should be," he wanted "the
Lily white . . . [to] in Love delight." None of this is
esoteric. Indeed, not only is it desperately human, it is also,
as I write, very contemporary once again, as we, too, worry
desperately about the effects of computerization, over-
industrialization, over-population, and mass-media-ization.
When Blake says he admires the tiger, when he asks "Did
he who made the Lamb make thee?", he is not making
pretty baubles for a tinselled Christmas tree. He is asking
basic questions, and expressing powerful social opinions.
Blake's society was perhaps a bit more used to having its
poets ask such questions, but fundamentally he was ignored: all his social influence has come only long after his
death—come, really, quite recently, only after World War
I reawakened us to some of the problems he dealt with, a
hundred and more years earlier.

And after Sigmund Freud, how can we mistake the profound seriousness and truth of this (also by Blake):

> I was angry with my friend:
> I told my wrath, my wrath did end.
> I was angry with my foe:
> I told it not, my wrath did grow.

> And I watered it in fears,
> Night and morning with my tears;
> And I sunned it with smiles,

And with soft deceitful wiles.

And it grew both day and night,
Till it bore an apple bright;
And my foe beheld it shine,
And he knew that it was mine,

And into my garden stole
When the night had veiled the pole:
In the morning glad I see
My foe outstretched beneath the tree.

We have special terminology, today, to explain what Blake here puts poetically. We talk about "repression" and "sublimation," about "transference" and "secondary hostility." It is simply another way of talking, however, and not a better way. Both ways are in fact necessary. To accomplish certain desirable things, psychology needs special terminology and the special meanings and concepts these terms convey. Poetry cannot and should not try to accomplish these particular things, no matter how desirable they may seem. But when someone is approached by a psychologist, and told about "repression" and "sublimation," and does not understand, he does not shout "Obscurity!" He bows to the expert, he humbles himself to Science and Learning. *But:* there is just as much Science and Learning, and for its time rather more Science and Learning, in Blake's poem about the poison tree, as there is in a learned paper in *The Journal of Experimental* (or *Clinical*) *Psychology.* They are not the same; each can learn, in part, from the other; neither should try to do without the other.

An alternative problem has developed, recently: the growing conviction among many people, especially younger people, that society itself is fast becoming meaningless, if it has not already died under its own weight. Poetry might just as well be meaningless too, in this view: people might just as well enjoy themselves, if and as they can, without worrying about outdated notions like meaning. A cheerful sequence of nice-sounding words, good words with pleasant, comforting vibrations—why shouldn't this be poetry, too?

If you are bound for the sun's empty plum
there is no need to mock the wine tongue
but if you are going to a rage of pennies
over a stevedore's wax ocean
then, remember: all long pajamas are frozen dust
unless an axe cuts my flaming grotto.

This is the opening of Philip Lamantia's "There are Many Pathways to the Garden," and it frankly tempts me to obscene comment. (One of my more printable reactions would run: "Better watch that axe in your grotto, man.") The spiritual father of this sort of thing, William Carlos Williams, is not often quite so emptily surrealistic as this—but he is often very nearly as aimless:

> . . . it fetches naked
> Indian
>
> women from a river
> Trumbull
>
> Varnum Henderson
> Frances
>
> Willard's corset is
> absurd—
>
> Banks White Columbus
> stretched
>
> in bed men felling trees
>
> The Hon. Michael
> C. Kerr
>
> onetime speaker of
> the House
>
> of Representatives
> Perry
>
> in a rowboat . . .

This extended passage is from Williams' "It is a Living Coral," a poem about the awfulness of official art. It seems to me very poor stuff. Good poetry, as I have tried to show, is not nearly so easy as this sort of thing makes it look.

And while there *is* sometimes obscurity in poetry, so too is there sometimes obscurity in everything men try to communicate to other men. When Beethoven's First Symphony was premièred, in Vienna, the critics were by and large horrified. "Only a mad man would use such harmonies!" they shouted. We listen to the same symphony, today, and hear a singularly mild piece of music, not fully developed Beethoven, imitative of Mozart and Haydn, and totally unobjectionable. But we have had, simply enough, the benefit of almost two hundred years of ear-training, of getting used to what Beethoven's early critics had no chance to get used to. Stravinsky's "Sacre du Printemps" (Rites of Spring) literally caused a riot, when it was premièred in Paris, just before World War I. There was such a bedlam of noise—people screaming, fighting, stamping—by the time the music was over, that although the orchestra had gone on playing, despite the riot, no one could hear a note, not even the conductor himself. This same Stravinsky score is played, today, at "fat-cat" concerts, for the least adventuresome and tamest of musical audiences. Matisse began as a wild man, a painter of blobs and smears (according to many critics); he died eminently respectable, working on commissions of church art. In short, as Wordsworth beautifully put it, a hundred and fifty years ago, in defending his own then-revolutionary poetry:

> Every author, as far as he is great and at the same time *original,* has had the task of *creating* the taste by which he is to be enjoyed: so has it been, so will it continue to be. . . . [For] of genius, in the fine arts, the only infallible sign is the widening of the sphere of human sensibility for the delight, honor, and benefit of human nature. . . . Is it to be supposed that the reader can make progress of this kind, like an Indian prince or general—stretched on his palanquin [a covered litter, carried on men's shoulders], and borne by slaves? No . . . the poet must reconcile himself, for a season, to few and scattered readers.

It is in fact hard to get used to something new, in short, and it is much easier to shrug your shoulders and say, "Oh the hell with it—it's only obscure raving." The loss is then a mutual one. *You* lose what the poet (the painter, the musician—any artist) has to tell you, the insights and the enrichments offered to society, throughout recorded time, by its artists. And the *poet,* if his society rejects him in his own lifetime, loses that sense of connection with his world which is potentially so valuable to him. And he loses, too, the support of that world, for no society does more than tolerate someone it considers "obscure" and unimportant. Every society makes mistakes; every society encourages some quacks, some just plain bad artists, and ignores some first-rate ones—usually, as I've said, because the first-rate artist presents an inherent difficulty, at first, which only time and habituation can overcome. It is of course hard to tell the quack from the genius, at times—but not nearly so hard as most people believe!

This is one side of the coin: *obscurity* as inherent difficulty, the difficulty of something new and different. There is of course the other side: *obscurity* as the artist's failure, the artist's inability to bring his work completely (and clearly) into focus.

> Fall off, ye garments of my misty weather,
> Drop from my eyes, ye scales of time's applying;
> Am I not godlike? meet not here together
> A past and future infinite, defying,
> The cold, still, callous moment of today?
> Am I not master of the calm alway?

This is the American writer, William Ellery Channing (a friend of Emerson and of Thoreau)—and if I had to answer his query, "Am I not master of the calm alway?", I would have to answer, very firmly, No, you're not—whatever "the calm alway" happens to be! I don't know what it is, and I do not know because Channing has not told me, though I suspect he thinks he has. This poetry is in part incoherent—and therefore obscure. The poet's capacity for clear expression, and also his capacity for clear thought *as a poet*, are not adequate to his theme. Later in the same long poem, titled "A Poet's Hope," Channing writes:

> O Time! O death! I clasp you in my arms,
> For I can soothe an infinite cold sorrow,
> And gaze contented on your icy charms . . .

I don't believe it for a moment.

But this is much less common, frankly, than most people —and certainly than most beginning readers of poetry— seem to believe. What seems to be obscurity, in a truly competent poet, is often something quite different. We may be too far separated from his time, and therefore from his cultural heritage and his automatic assumptions about the universe and men. Milton is often, for beginning readers of poetry, a poet of this sort. More sheer information is needed, than the beginner—in our time—is apt to have. But information can be acquired, really quite easily—and the poetry is still there, waiting, once you have the information, waiting just as it has always been. Or, just as likely, we may not have entirely understood the way in which the particular poet (or the particular poetic culture) works, how this poetic mind operates. This is often the case with new poetry in our own culture: early readers of Dylan Thomas had exactly this problem. But once we do succeed in understanding how the poetic mind works, the obscurity vanishes—because, in fact, it has been more in us than in the poetry. Or, perhaps more accurately, it has been in an imperfect blending of ourselves and the poet—for, really, does poetry or any other art fully exist without some kind of audience? What is music if no one listens? Painting, if no one looks? Poetry, if no one reads?

Most apparent obscurity falls into one or another of the categories I have been discussing. I do not mean that good poets are perfect: not at all. What I do mean is that they are superbly intelligent men, with enormous gifts of expression and interpretation, and we are less than fair both to ourselves and to them if we do not give them credit for this intelligence, if we do not try to understand just what it is that we think we cannot understand. Give the good poet the benefit of the doubt, and he will give you more than that, in return.

CHAPTER FOUR: The Shape of Poems

I don't want even to try to meet the old challenge: can form and content be separated? The only answer I want to give is a firm "Yes," and an equally firm "No." On the highest of levels, form is content, and content is form. At the same time, for purposes of analysis—certain kinds of analysis—either form or content can be talked about separately, one from the other. It does not matter, really, so long as you remember what it is you're doing. If you think that by counting the lines or the rhymes in a poem, you have said all there is to be said, then you're obviously not operating validly. But if you limit the scope of your analysis—two imperfect rhymes do *not* equal a philosophical stance, and an irregular caesura (pause) does *not* equal an emotional bias—the particular perspective you assume is not I think of much importance.

I am not going to talk about meter, in this chapter: that will come in chapter five. I want, here, to discuss some of the more common and more significant structural forms: (1) couplets; (2) ballads and hymns; (3) sonnets; (4) songs; (5) dialogues and monologues; (6) narratives; and (7) discursive free forms. This is not intended to be an exhaustive discussion; it is intended to represent those forms which virtually all poets writing in English have used, and it is also intended to represent the great majority of poems by these same poets. The fact that Shelley's "Ode to the West Wind" is written in *terza rima* (an intricately rhyme-linked form, borrowed from the Italian, and especially from Dante), for example, is less significant, for my purposes here, than the fact that it is virtually the only viable exemplar of the form in our language. Nor will I here discuss those elaborate and challenging forms which some, and often many poets like to play with, like the palindrome (reading the same backwards as it does forward), or the triolet (an elaborately repetitive form, derived from French usage). Similarly, forms which are basically part of other poetic cultures—like the Malay/Indonesian *pantun,* or the Urdu *ghazal*—are not here discussed, though they have had their adherents, especially among contemporary poets.

(1) *Couplets*

A couplet is not the smallest possible form, though it occupies only two lines. There are a number of one-line forms, epigrams (usually but not necessarily satirical), epitaphs (tombstone writing), and poems which are just plain one-line poems. Guy Davenport, an excellent translator, has used one-line and even one-word poems in his versions of the ancient Greek poets Sappho and Archilochus, both of whose work survives only in badly-torn manuscripts and fragmentary quotations embedded in other people's books. Davenport's Archilochus #71, for example, reads:

> Greet insolence with outrage.

His Archilochus #61 reads:

> Ass kisser!

And #89 reads, simply:

> Plums.

And his Sappho #168 reads:

> And night's black sleep upon the eyes.

None of these were intended to be whole poems, at least as originally written in Greek. In Davenport's translations they clearly are meant to be poems—fragmentary, but poems for all that—and I think they succeed. But it is just as important, here, to note that the attempt was made.

The couplet form—two lines, usually but not necessarily rhyming—offers the poet much more than twice as much room as does the single-line form:

> Seven wealthy towns contend for Homer dead
> Through which the living Homer begged his bread.

This anonymous little poem, slightly uncertain metrically, and by no means brilliantly expressed, nevertheless has real force and effect. The unknown poet is plainly not capable of the sophisticated compression of Davenport's "Greet insolence with outrage"—but so powerful, so pithy, is the *form* itself that the couplet here reproduced has vectors pushing out in all sorts of directions, artistic, social, and moral. In a sense, then, the form is not only sustaining, is not only a challenge to the writer's best efforts, it is even *by its very nature as a form* a kind of artistic accomplishment, almost a kind of guarantee of merit. If the artist is capable of bringing it off, even imperfectly, he thereby enters on a plane of achievement which is created, in good part, by form rather than by content. (Again, the two are of course on the highest levels inseparable.) A totally inept portrait painter is laughed at—but an unpolished, even a crude portrait painter who nevertheless catches something of his subject, is generally acknowledged to have accomplished something quite real and distinctly worthy. An even more satisfactory analogy is, in music, the string quartet form. Singularly bare and stripped-down, especially for the composer accustomed to thinking in terms of orchestral color—accustomed, indeed, to relying on orchestral color—the string quartet virtually forces the composer to fall back on more solid and essential musical elements than mere tone color. (Edvard Grieg, a noted colorist, and generally a second- or third-ranking composer, wrote one work of incontestable genius—and that was, of course, his one string quartet.)

THE NEW CAKE OF SOAP
Lo, how it gleams and glistens in the sun
Like the cheek of a Chesterton.

IN A STATION OF THE METRO   [metro-the Paris subway]
The apparition of these faces in the crowd;
Petals on a wet, black bough.

SALVATIONISTS: I
Come, my songs, let us speak of perfection—
We shall get ourselves rather disliked.

These three little poems, all by Ezra Pound—one of the great technicians of modern poetry, and in some ways perhaps the greatest translator of all time—show something of the range of the form. The first, "The New Cake of Soap," is delightfully nasty; if not exactly malicious, neither is it entirely friendly. (I have often wondered, inconclusively, if Pound intended to pun on "cheek"—which in a secondary meaning is synonymous with "buttock.") The second poem, "In a Station of the Metro," shows that a couplet need not depend on wit: its concision can be that of a beautifully integrated poem, condensed into an almost fiercely precise image. And the dry conversational tone of the third poem, "Salvationists: I," shows how easy (smooth) and supple the couplet can be, how well adapted to virtually any stance. Significantly, for modern practice, only one of these three couplets by Pound is in rhyme—although crowd/bough, arguably, is at least a part-rhyme. (What it really is, of course, is *assonance*, or vowel-rhyme.)

Balance, concision, and contrast are the basic stuff of virtually all couplets. The poet either amplifies, in line two, what he has called to our attention in line one (as in "In a Station of the Metro"), or else he poses the second line against the first (as in "The New Cake of Soap"). In either case, the secret of the form is always to pivot at the right moment, not to lean too heavily at either end—and to avoid, above all, any sense that concision is a strain on the poet's capacities. Ben Jonson, for example, is a superbly witty writer, whose epigrams—relatively short, and almost always nasty—are justly famous. Jonson is however not entirely comfortable in the couplet form; it seems *too* stripped-down for him, he becomes awkward:

> TO THE READER
> Pray thee, take care, that tak'st my book in hand,
> To read it well: that is, to understand.

This is distinctly lame stuff. There is too much to the first half of the poem—and not enough to the second half. Jonson does not leave himself room to do, in the second line, what must be done in order for the form to work. I would prefer this poem had Jonson written something more like this:

> Careful, reader, my book is in thy hand:
> To read it well, thou first must understand.

This strips away the awkward "that is," of Jonson's second line: the writer of couplets hasn't room to be awkward in! By introducing "careful," this revision also simplifies the syntax of the first half of the poem and allows the second line a syntax of its own. "That is, to understand," is little more than a desperate gasp, as the poem whirls by, a frantic attempt to squeeze in—quick, before it's too late! —the point of the whole thing.

Ben Jonson's only couplet-epigram of real merit, I think, is his "To the Alchemists":

> If all you boast of your great art be true,
> Sure, willing poverty lives most in you.

And I would be tempted to speculate that it was Jonson's use of the iambic pentameter, as opposed to the iambic tetrameter line, which limited his couplets, if I did not know many other couplets in this same iambic pentameter metric, but with far more grace and power. (Meter, once again, is discussed in chapter five.)

A LAME BEGGAR
I am unable, yonder beggar cries,
To stand, or move; if he say true, he *lies*.

ON JOAN
Joan would go tell her hairs; and well   [go tell-count]
    she might,
Having but seven in all, three black, four white.

EPITAPH, INTENDED FOR SIR ISAAC NEWTON, IN
    WESTMINSTER ABBEY
Nature, and Nature's Laws, lay hid in Night.
God said, *Let Newton be!* and All was *Light*.

These three couplets are, in this order, by John Donne, Robert Herrick, and Alexander Pope. Note that the turning-point, the moment of pivot, is not necessarily the same thing as the end of a line. In "A Lame Beggar" the pivot comes well into the second line. In "On Joan" it comes in the middle of the first line. There is no inevitable shortness of breath, caused by a run-over (enjambed) line: Ben Jonson, as I said, brings his trouble on himself. Note, in these last-quoted couplets, how Donne's fondness for puns carries into every form he employs; how Herrick deliciously postpones his climax, hinting at it with "Having but seven in all," but then topping that with "three black, four white" (and all that this says about Joan's age—and her state of health—and her morals, it being "the French pox," or syphilis, which caused hair to fall out); and how Pope, in only two lines, has compressed a remarkable grandness and intensity.

Pope, in fact, is not only a master, but probably *the* master of the couplet form. (There have been and I suspect still are critics who argue that his poems are little more than a tissue of independent or semi-related couplets, sewn willy-nilly together. No one who has read, say, the splendidly integrated, wonderfully consecutive "Epistle to Dr. Arbuthnot," can believe this.) Pope's neatest couplet, perhaps, is that entitled "Epigram, Engraved on the Collar of a Dog which I gave to his Royal Highness":

> I am his Highness' Dog at Kew;
> Pray tell me, Sir, whose Dog are you?

Taken just as a poem about dogs, this is fine stuff—but once the extra dimension is grasped, the sly dig at tame, subservient *men* (with the nature of tame, subservient dogs), the couplet becomes really extraordinarily fine.

I have been talking about the couplet, so far, as an independent form. It is also a subordinate form: two joined couplets can constitute the form known as the *quatrain* (that is, a poem, or a part of a poem, having four lines). And the couplet serves, also, in such other larger forms as the Shakespearian sonnet (see section three of this chapter, below), rhyme royal (a seven-line stanza, in iambic pentameter, rhyming A B A B B C C), and the Spenserian stanza (nine iambic lines, rhyming A B A B B C B C C). As a subordinate form, the couplet preserves to a very large degree a special kind of autonomy, especially when it is rhymed: it is difficult to avoid becoming aware of its existence as a couplet, even when it is embedded in a larger form. Shakespeare's *Romeo and Juliet*, for example, is a full-length drama, but when a scene ends with a rhymed couplet, the couplet-nature of the subform is very plain:

> [Romeo]   Show me a mistress that is
>   passing fair,   [passing-surpassing]
>   What doth her beauty serve but as a note
>   Where I may read who passed that passing
>   fair?   [passed-surpassed; fair-woman]
>   Farewell. That canst not teach me to for-
>   get.
> [Benvolio]   I'll pay that doctrine, or else die in debt.

Several scenes further on in the play:

> [Servant]   Madam, the guests are come, supper served up,
>   you called, my young lady asked for, the nurse
>   cursed in the pantry, and everything in ex-
>   tremity. I must hence to wait. I beseech you,
>   follow straight.
> [Mother]   We follow thee. Juliet, the County   [the County-
>   stays.   her intended husband]
> [Nurse]   Go, girl, seek happy nights to happy days.

An odd extension of the couplet, used mostly by seventeenth- and eighteenth-century poets, is the *triplet*. Here is one by John Dryden:

> That Sting enfixed within her haughty Mind,
> The downfall of her Empire she divined,
> And her proud Heart with secret Sorrow pined.

Never terribly popular—Pope used it much less often than did Dryden—the triplet is almost more an extended couplet than a form in its own right. The triple rhyme—unlike the couplet, the triplet always rhymes—distinctly weakens that pithy, incisive thrust which makes the couplet proper so useful a form.

The "heroic" (or "end-stopped") couplet almost needs to be discussed as a separate form. I have said that the couplet in general is simply a two-line form, which may or may not rhyme. There is also no necessary metrical pattern for the general couplet form. Nor does the general couplet form need to be end-stopped—that is, there is no rule against enjambement, running over from one couplet to another, or from a subordinated couplet to whatever else may follow it. But the heroic couplet is a completely different animal. It is almost always end-stopped, it always rhymes, and it is always in iambic pentameter. The form is not much used today, except for mock-heroic or satirical poetry, but it has been enormously popular and I suspect will never entirely fall out of favor—it fits so beautifully with the nature of the language. Again, Pope is *the* master of the form. Here is a random sampling, from assorted poems:

> 'Tis hard to say, if greater Want of Skill   [want-lack]
> Appear in *Writing* or in Judging *ill.*   [ill-badly]

> And, spite of Pride, in erring Reason's spite,
> One truth is clear, "Whatever IS, is RIGHT."

> Know then thyself, presume not God to scan:
> The proper study of Mankind is Man.

> So well-bred Spaniels
>   civilly delight   [civilly-politely, gently]
> In mumbling of the Game[mumbling-toothless cheering]
>   they dare not bite.

> Of all mad Creatures, if the Learned are right,
> It is the Slaver [slobber] kills, and not the Bite.

> To happy Convents, bosomed   [bosomed-enclosed]
>   deep in vines,
> Where slumber Abbots, purple as their wines.

Pope can be quoted for pages—but he is not the only writer of perfect heroic couplets:

> At last he rose and twitched his mantle   [twitched-tied]
> blue:
> Tomorrow to fresh woods, and pastures new.

This is the concluding couplet to Milton's "Lycidas," a poem not written exclusively in heroic couplets, but which makes good use of the form. Thomas Wolfe took the title of his most famous (and his best) novel from another of the heroic couplets in "Lycidas":

> Look homeward Angel, now, and melt with
> ruth,   [ruth-pity]
> And O ye Dolphins, waft the hapless youth.   [waft-carry]

Byron relished the form:

> Oh Southey! Southey! cease thy varied song!
> A bard may chant too often and too long.
>
> • • •
>
> The babe unborn thy dread intent may rue: [rue-regret]
> "God help thee," Southey, and thy readers too.

Edward Fitzgerald's immensely popular *Rubáiyát of Omar Khayyám* often uses the heroic couplet to begin a quatrain:

> I sometimes think that never blows so red
> The Rose as where some buried Caesar bled;
>
> Oh, threats of Hell and Hopes of Paradise!
> One thing at least is certain—*This* life flies;
>
> Indeed, indeed, Repentance oft before
> I swore—but was I sober when I swore?

What these examples show, I think, is the extraordinary variety of this brief form, the number of variations that can be wrung from its apparently closely confining boundaries. This is principally a matter of subtle but very noticeable changes in rhythm. In the two heroic couplets from "Lycidas," for example, Milton uses two sharply distinct rhythms:

> At last he rose [PAUSE] and twitched his mantle blue
>   [PAUSE]:
> Tomorrow to fresh woods [PAUSE], and pastures
>   new [PAUSE].

Look homeward Angel [PAUSE], now [PAUSE], and
                          melt with ruth [PAUSE],
And O ye Dolphins [PAUSE], waft the hapless youth
                          [PAUSE].

Without using very complicated notation, and I have no
intention of using it anywhere in this book, I cannot
indicate just exactly *how* subtle these pauses are, much
subtler than they seem. I can note, however, that the pause
after "now," in the second couplet, is clearly a shorter
pause than that after "ruth," at the end of the same line—
but, equally clearly, is a longer pause than that after
"Angel," again in the same line. If this seems hyper-
subtle, so attenuated as to be insignificant, think, please, of
the difference between the piano styles of Chopin and of
Liszt. Listz had large hands, and great strength, and
smashed away at the keyboard: his loud notes were louder
than anyone else's—but his soft notes were louder than
anyone else's, too. And this was all right, because the whole
scale of his playing was large and loud. But Chopin did
not have powerful hands. His loud notes were softer than
anyone else's. And, again, his soft notes were softer than
anyone else's—so that this too was all right, since the
whole scale of *his* playing was small and soft. That is, the
whole thing is relative. An epic poet has to have a large
voice and leather lungs; a poet who uses the heroic couplet
does not tend to bellow. As Pope puts it—and in the
heroic couplet, who better to say the last word?—in his
"On a Lady Who Pissed at the Tragedy Of Cato: Oc-
casioned by an Epigram on a Lady Who Wept at It":

> While maudlin Whigs deplored their Cato's Fate,
> Still with dry eyes the Tory Celia sate,
> But while her Pride forbids her Tears to flow,
> The gushing Waters find a Vent below:
> Though secret, yet with copious Grief she mourns,
> Like twenty River-Gods with all their Urns.
> Let others screw their Hypocritic Face,
> She shows her grief in a sincerer Place;
> There Nature reigns, and Passion void of Art,
> For that Road leads directly to the Heart.

("There Nature *reigns*" is a pun that must have delighted
Pope: read "rains" for "reigns." The even more delicate
pun on "void"—"to void" meaning "to urinate or to def-
ecate"—must have tickled him silly—and I for one don't
blame him!)

(2) *Ballads and Hymns*

Ballads and hymns are the poetic forms most familiar to most people; they need the least amount of comment and explanation. Both are, in a sense, folk forms, and I have linked them in this section because they are technically similar. (Their subject matter is of course very often different—but this is a chapter on form, not on content.)

from a hymn:

A mighty fortress is our God.
    A bulwark never failing;
Our helper He amid the flood
    Of mortal ills prevailing.

from a ballad:

And it's fare you well, my dearest dear,
    And it's fare you well for ever,
And if you don't go with me now,
    Don't let me see you never.

Hymns and ballads are both oral forms, both of them meant to be sung rather than read—which probably accounts for their regular beat (four stresses in one line, followed by three in the next), and the strong rhymes of the even-numbered lines. Both hymns and ballads are usually written in quatrains; there is usually a pause at the end of the second line, thus dividing the quatrain, in effect, into two couplets. Nor is this simply an enumeration of dry technical characteristics: the division of each quatrain into two couplets is basic to the form. The general rule is that hymns and ballads advance like children playing king of the hill, one step forward, one step back. That is, whatever is said in the first line of a quatrain, is essentially repeated in the second line; whatever is said in the third line, is essentially repeated in the fourth line. The unit of expression, accordingly, is the couplet, not the line. "A mighty fortress is our God," says line one, and line two changes "fortress" to "bulwark" and "mighty" to "never failing." He is our "helper," says line three, "amid the flood"—which is then explained, in line four, as the "mortal ills" (for which obviously we need help) which "prevail" (like the "flood" they are). The ballad stanza I have quoted works in exactly the same way. Line one says good-bye, line two says good-bye for ever. Line three says come with me, and line four says or else stay where you are.

Several additional examples will help to make this pro-

cess clearer. Again, here is first a hymn stanza, and then a
ballad stanza:

> O holy Child of Bethlehem!
>   Descend to us, we pray;
> Cast out our sin, and enter in,
>   Be born in us today.

> Will ye go to the Highlands, Leezie Lindsay?
>   Will ye go to the Highlands wi me?
> Will ye go to the Highlands, Leezie Lindsay,
>   My pride and my darling to be?

The first couplet of the hymn (that is, lines one and two)
invokes the "holy child"; the second couplet explains why.
The invocation of "O holy Child of Bethlehem" is not
substantively added to by "descend to us, we pray," though,
of course, the two lines are not identical and, equally
plainly, there is an increment of some sort in spelling out
the fact that the invoking party wants Christ to "descend."
Basically, however, line two is only a minor variation on
line one; the idea of Christ descending is implicit in calling
out to him. Similarly, to "cast out our sin" in line
three implies, very clearly, the incarnation specified in line
four, "be born in us today."

This patterning is too clear, in the ballad stanza, to need
any comment.

The process is reminiscent of the old joke about the
world-famous, universally successful preacher. Asked his
secret, he replies: "It's very simple. First I tell them what
I'm going to tell them. Then I tell them. Then I tell them
what I've told them." Oral forms virtually demand this
kind of patient progress; the listener is otherwise likely to
be left behind, uncomprehending. Every link in an oral
chain must be perceived, must be understood, for the
listener to follow at all—and since the ear is the receiving
organ, not the eye, everything must be pretty much instantly
comprehensible. When hymns or ballads become a *written*
form, accordingly, they become far more complex—and
no longer singable. Consider John Donne's "A Hymn to
God the Father":

> Wilt thou forgive that sin where I begun,
>   Which was my sin, though it were done before?
> Wilt thou forgive that sin, through which I run,
>   And do run still; though still I do deplore?
> When thou hast done, thou hast not done,
>   For I have more.

The hymn form itself has vanished; so, too, has the simple repetitiveness of the true hymn. Donne's "hymn" is a poem, and a very beautiful poem: the pun on his own name (done/Donne) is delicately persuasive—on the page. It might be turned, by a clever enough composer, into an interesting art-song. But a singing hymn? Even George Herbert, whose style seems to me better suited to the writing of true hymns, does not write a truly singable hymn, though he was devoted both to the form and to religious poetry generally. He does not produce a singing hymn, indeed, even when he titles his poem, carefully, "A True Hymn":

> My joy, my life, my crown!
> My heart was meaning all the day,
>   Somewhat it fain would say: [fain would-wanted to]
> And still it runneth muttering up and down
> With only this, "My joy, my life, my crown."

This is usually what happens, also, to the literary, as opposed to the true, ballad: it becomes simply another poem, usually lyrical, but not distinctive from other written forms. Here is the opening of Byron's "Ballad, To the Tune of 'Sally in Our Alley' ":

> Of all the twice ten thousand bards
>   That ever penned a canto,
> Whom Pudding or whom Praise rewards
>   For lining a portmanteau . . .

These lines don't repay analysis; it's not a very good poem. The point is, however, that this is *eye*-poetry, not *ear*-balladry. Simple repetitiveness has given way to complicated language and literary allusions. John Donne's deservedly famous pun on done/Donne is indeed totally dependent on the eye seeing the two words, for to the ear they are one word, and quite indistinguishable.

I do not mean to suggest that no *poet* can write either a true hymn or a true ballad. I do not even mean to suggest that all true hymns and ballads must inevitably follow the basic forms here discussed. But most true hymns and ballads *do* follow these forms. And most poets cannot (and *do not*) write true hymns or ballads.

(3) Sonnets

The sonnet is the most formal of all the commonly used (and popular) poetic forms. There are many possible variants, but the almost invariable trademarks are length, fourteen lines; meter, iambic pentameter; close rhyming; and carefully structured internal divisions, usually with form and content coordinated. Originally an Italian form (*sonetto,* "little song"), the sonnet has spread to every European language (Pushkin's friend, Baron Delvig, domesticated it in Russian) and to most non-European ones (it reached Indonesian poetry in 1918). Its popularity is easy to understand: it is short; it is both lyrical and, if the poet so chooses, philosophical or descriptive, even narrative (especially in a sequence of linked sonnets, usually called a "sonnet series"); it provides at one and the same time both a firm foundation on which to build and a technical challenge of immense appeal; and by now it is so well established, in so many poetic traditions, that it has become something like painting in oils, or sculpting in marble, or playing Chopin if one is a pianist, or playing Paganini if one is a violinist.

There are three principal kinds of sonnets in English: Petrarchan (or Italian), Shakespearian, and Spenserian. I want to discuss them under those headings and in that order.

Sonnets: Italian

Italian being a rhyme-rich language, a language in which, indeed, it is almost harder not to rhyme than it is to rhyme, the Italian sonnet form naturally makes elaborate use of rhyme. Divided into two main parts, one of eight lines (the octave), the second of six lines (the sestet), it is rhymed A B B A A B B A in the octave, C D E C D E and sometimes C D C D C D in the sestet. The form is stately, lyrical, even majestic; it is no accident that one of the greatest advocates of the Italian sonnet is John Milton, perhaps the stateliest of all English poets. His noblest sonnets are too complex to be set out here, where form rather than substance is our concern, but his "Sonnet 9," if not his greatest, shows at least the grace with which he handles the form:

Lady, that in the prime of earliest youth
    Wisely hast shunned the broad way and the green
    And with those few art eminently seen
    That labor up the hill of heavenly Truth,
The better part with Mary and with Ruth
    Chosen thou hast, and they that
      overween   [overween-act arrogant]

And at thy growing virtues
    fret their spleen   [fret-gnaw; spleen-spite]
No anger find in thee, but pity and ruth.   [ruth-sorrow]
Thy care is fixed and zealously attends
    To fill thy odorous lamp with   [odorous-fragrant]
        deeds of light
And Hope that reaps not shame. Therefore be sure
Thou, when the Bridegroom with his feastful friends
    Passes to bliss at the mid hour of night,
    Hast gained thy entrance, Virgin wise and pure.

(The Biblical reference, in the sestet, is to Matthew 25: 1–
13, which tells how the wise virgins had their lamps filled
in advance, and were ready for Christ the Bridegroom,
when he came at midnight. The foolish virgins, however,
had delayed, and were not prepared.) This deeply religious
poem is a kind of testimonial, a statement of support and
encouragement for a woman who has chosen a difficult path
and who is meeting with considerable criticism, with strong
social and perhaps family pressure against her chosen way.
There is no evidence about who in fact the lady was, or
how Milton came to know her, but the human impulse
seems clear: Milton was pained at her pain, under fire,
and wanted to help, wanted to confirm her in her decision
by adding the force of his own approval. The poem's structure is extremely simple. Lines one through four, the first
half of the octave, say that she has chosen the minority
way, but the best way. Lines five through eight, concluding
the octave, say again that hers is the best way, and point
out that even spiteful critics make her react gently and
with kindness, and do not make her angry. This then is
the situation: the octave's job is to set out what *is*, leaving
it for the sestet to round this off with a prediction, or with
some different, some wider perspective. The sestet says, for
the third time, that the lady's choice is a superlatively
good one, affirming in strong terms that when the Day of
Judgment comes she will be found among the blessed, not
among the damned.

This is an outline of the close fusion between form and
substance, in Italian sonnets of this sort. It is a still subtler
fusion, however. The switching back and forth, in the
octave, between its two rhymes, *-uth* and *-een*, is handled
so as to stress, in turn, the forward motion of the poem's
substance. The rhyme for "youth," for example, hangs
fire until line four, when it closes, powerfully, with "truth"
—and is immediately reemphasized by "Ruth," in line five.

Whereupon the *-uth* rhyme hangs fire (or seems, rather, almost to disappear) until line eight, when "ruth" brings it quietly and decisively back. (This is Milton taking advantage of the form, please note, and not Milton inventing the form. This is part of what I mean by my claim, above, that the sonnet offers poets both a firm foundation and a technical challenge. The form is only an empty box, until properly filled; the poet must fill it properly, but he does not need to worry about the shape of the box.) The inside rhymes of the octave (that is, lines two and three, six and seven—which I call "inside" because they are in each case surrounded by the "outside" rhymes of lines one and four, and five and eight) are in fairly sharp contrast, using the high, tight vowel phonemically represented as /iy/ instead of the back, rounded vowel /uw/ (as in "truth" and "youth"). I don't want to make too much of the psychological significance of this difference in sound, but it is a real thing, even if it is not always a clear, or certainly not a major, force in poetry. (It is in some ways parallel to the distinction, in psychological terms, between major and minor keys in music.) Both "green" and "seen," though words with favorable connotations, have a taut, even a tense aura which in fact contrasts with the open ease of "youth" and "truth"—and the other two inside rhymes, "overween" and "spleen," both of them words with unfavorable connotations, are in even sharper contrast.

The subtlest effects, in the Italian sonnet, often occur in the sestet, where (and especially with the preferred rhyme scheme, C D E C D E) the rhymes are more spread out, more diffused. In Milton's sonnet no rhyme, in the sestet, is closer to its paired word than three lines. It is not easy, perhaps, to sense the difference which this makes—but surely it is not hard to see the difference between, say:

> Roses are red,
> And violets are blue,
> Candy is sweet,
> And so are you,

and a stretched-out version, with spread-out rhymes, which might go like this:

> Roses are red,
> And violets are blue,
> Candy is sweet,
> And sugar is nice,
> And so are you.

The blue/you rhyme simply does not have the same effect, in the second version. It's not that the second version is inferior: it is just different, quieter, subtler. Which kind of effect he will use, depends on what the poet wants to do. Some poets—Milton included—find the C D E C D E form of the sestet sometimes too quiet, too rhyme-thin, and therefore employ one or more of the patterns with closer rhyme:

> ... vested all in white, pure as her mind:
> Her face was veiled, yet to my fancied sight
> Love, sweetness, goodness in her person shined
> So clear, as in no face with more delight.
> But O as to embrace me she inclined,   [inclined-bent]
> I waked, she fled, and day brought back my night.

> ... In our walls is hung
> Armory of the invincible Knights of old:
> We must be free or die, who speak the tongue
> That Shakespeare spake; the faith and morals hold
> Which Milton held.—In everything we are sprung
> Of Earth's first blood, have titles manifold.

The first example is by Milton, the second by Wordsworth. Milton rhymes, here, C D C D C D: this is much richer, and at the same time much less subtle, than C D E C D E. Wordsworth rhymes his sestet C D C D C D, avoiding the final heroic couplet but still employing stronger, and less subtle, rhyming. With only two rhymes in the sestet, instead of three, the rhymes seem to keep coming back, over and over, and we cannot help but be much more aware of them.

This capacity for small but almost endless variation, within a small and (to the nonpoet's eye) apparently fixed and immutable form, is yet another source of the sonnet's perpetual fascination. I think I can perhaps best indicate the form's flexibility by closing this section on the Italian sonnet with Keats' delicately comic "To a Cat." It doesn't seem to be very well known; I have always found it delightful—and technically an immense tour-de-force. The octave is in standard Italian sonnet pattern; the sestet is rhymed as in the example from Wordsworth—but how different the tone!

> Cat! who hast passed thy grand
>   climacteric,   [i.e., reached old age]
> How many mice and rats hast in thy days
> Destroyed?—How many tid-bits stolen? Gaze

With those bright languid segments green, and prick
Those velvet ears—but prithee do not stick
   Thy latent talons in me—and upraise
   Thy gentle mew—and tell me all thy frays
Of fish and mice, and rats and tender chick:
   Nay, look not down, nor lick thy dainty wrists
For all the wheezy asthma—and for all
Thy tail's tip is nicked off—and though the fists
   Of many a maid has given thee many a maul,
Still in that fur as soft as when the lists
   In youth thou enterd'st on glass-bottled wall.

("The lists" refers to the tourneys in which knights fought. Keats masterfully crosses this ancient and courtly image with the backalley/large city image of "glass-bottled wall" —that is, walls in which slabs of sharp broken bottle glass have been set, point upward, to repel intruders and thieves, and along which cats engage in *their* "knightly" combat.)

Sonnets: Shakespearian

The Shakespearian sonnet is different from the Italian in two basic ways, rhyme-pattern and structural division. Both of these differences involve matters of form and of content. The Shakespearian sonnet has four basic component parts, instead of two: three quatrains, followed by a heroic couplet. Each quatrain is separately rhymed, as is the couplet. The rhyme-pattern is A B A B   C D C D   E F E F G G. Shakespeare did not invent the form (probably the Earl of Surrey did); he did perfect and popularize it.

That time of year thou mayst in me behold
When yellow leaves, or none, or few, do hang
Upon those boughs which shake against the cold,
Bare ruined choirs where late   [late-lately]
   the sweet birds sang.
In me thou see'st the twilight of such day
As after sunset fadeth in the West,
Which by-and-by black night doth take away,
Death's second self, that seals up all in rest.
In me thou see'st the glowing of such fire
That on the ashes of his youth doth lie,
As the deathbed whereon it must expire,
Consumed with that which it was nourished by.
   This thou perceivest, which makes thy love more
      strong,
   To love that well which thou must leave ere long.

("Choirs," in line four, refers to that part of a church called the "choir." After Henry VIII's forced and sometimes violent disestablishment of the Church, there were many "bare ruined choirs" in England.)

The most obvious difference between the Shakespearian and Italian forms is, I think, the variant rhyme-patternings —motivated, as I've said, in good part by the much greater difficulty of finding rhymes in English. But I do not think this the most significant difference. The division into four (rather than two) component parts seems to me a much more basic alteration, since it encourages the poet to think more in developmental than in descriptive terms. That is, in the Italian sonnet a situation is described (the octave) and then pointed or resolved (the sestet). It is a fairly gentle kind of approach, and the rhyming too tends to be relatively gentle. But in the Shakespearian sonnet the poet frames not one but *three* statements, and then caps them with a concise, often an epigrammatic couplet. The three statements are usually (though not invariably) clearly separated one from the other. In practice, they tend to become a sequence, a set of developmental rather than merely descriptive statements. This fits the quatrain form more naturally than it does the octave; the A B A B rhyming also helps support a developmental approach. And in order to build toward, to prepare the reader for, the capping couplet, the three quatrains further tend to become more challenging statements, more dramatic. In a word, then, the Italian sonnet tends to be more meditative, while the Shakespearian sonnet tends to be bolder and brighter.

And this affects all the component parts of the poem. Without pressing a detailed and word-by-word analysis and comparison, I think it is not hard to see that the Shakespeare sonnet, just quoted, uses starker, more sharply-etched images than the Milton sonnet. For example, "labor up the hill of heavenly Truth" (Milton) and "Bare ruined choirs where late the sweet birds sang" (Shakespeare), or "Thy care is fixed and zealously attends/ To fill thy odorous lamp with deeds of light" (Milton) and "In me thou see'st the glowing of such fire/ That on the ashes of his youth doth lie" (Shakespeare). Milton's music, too, is a longer, more relaxed affair: Shakespeare's music is tauter, crisper. The gorgeous suspensions of Shakespeare's second line— "yellow leaves (PAUSE), or none (PAUSE), or few (PAUSE), do hang . . ."—would not fit in Milton's poem. (I must add that this Shakespearian line seems to me one of the most brilliantly virtuosic in all of English poetry, fantastically daring and marvellously successful.) The long, full breaths of Milton's lines would have no room in the tight-packed quatrains of Shakespeare's poem. A more evaluative comparison would be unfair, because I have chosen one of the greatest of Shakespeare's sonnets and, as I've said, I have not been able to choose one of Milton's best sonnets. But all the same, without drawing any conclusions as to which is the better sonneteer, it is easy to draw conclusions as to the different things each man is up to. There are, appropriately, more contrasts in Shakespeare. Both poems have fine balance, but Shakespeare balances in shorter spaces, and Milton's balance is, again, a longer and larger-scaled affair. Precision, too, is of a different sort in the two sonnets: Milton's precision is low-keyed, Shakespeare's stands in bright spotlights and is painted in strong colors. Which you write, and which you read, depends on who you are and what you want.

Keats more often used the Italian than the Shakespearian form, but one of his greatest sonnets is in the Shakespearian form (with the couplet, however, not being a heroic couplet, not end-stopped, but beginning in line twelve and running over—making for a rather more Italianate effect, at the close):

> When I have fears that I may cease to be
>   Before my pen has gleaned my teeming brain,
> Before high piled books,
>   in charactry,   [charactry-symbolic representation]
>   Hold like rich garners   [garner-storehouse]
>   the full-ripened grain;
> When I behold, upon the night's starred face,
>   Huge cloudy symbols of a high romance,
> And think that I may never live to trace
>   Their shadows, with the magic hand of chance;
> And when I feel, fair creature of an hour!
>   That I shall never look upon thee more,
> Never have relish in the faery power
>   Of unreflecting love;—then on the shore
> Of the wide world I stand alone, and think
> Till Love and Fame to nothingness do sink.

Like the Shakespeare sonnet, quoted earlier, this is a love poem—but how much difference two hundred years have made! The second quatrain, in particular, seems to me almost a definition of that ill-defined literary movement, Romanticism: "huge cloudy symbols of a high romance."

The three quatrains are distinctly developmental. The first quatrain is most descriptive; the second elaborates on the loss which has been postulated in the opening lines; and the third quatrain makes that hypothetical but threatening loss terribly personal and poignant. The extended couplet then caps this sequence with an image of large meditativeness, almost cosmic in tone.

Alexander Pope seems never to have written a sonnet—or not preserved it, if he did write one—but in most periods the sonnet has held a place in English poetry. It still does. Robert Lowell's *Notebook 1967–68* is entirely written in a variant of the sonnet form; Yeats and Auden have written fine sonnets; the great Indonesian poet, Chairil Anwar, has some superb sonnets. I have two in my own first book of poems, one in my second, and there is already one in the notebook which will eventually be my third collection. Like the novel, the sonnet is always being criticized, its death is always being announced. But to plagiarize Mark Twain, reports of its death are considerably exaggerated.

Sonnets: Spenserian

Least popular of the three major sonnet forms, the Spenserian sonnet is a kind of compromise between the Italian and the Shakespearian forms. It has three quatrains and a couplet, but the rhymes are interlinked, between quatrains, instead of being separate. The rhyme-pattern is A B A B B C B C C D C D E E. Strictly it is not really a form in its own right so much as an Italian-oriented variation on the Shakespearian form. I do not think it needs much comment. Here then is Spenser's sonnet, *Amoretti* # 30, which shows the form quite nicely:

My love is like to ice, and I to fire:
>How comes it then that this her cold so great
>Is not dissolv'd through my so hot desire,
>But harder grows the more I her entreat?
Or how comes it that my exceeding heat
>Is not delayed by her heart, frozen cold—
>But that I burn much more in boiling sweat,
>And feel my flames augmented manifold?
What more miraculous thing may be told
>That fire which all things melts, should harden ice.
>And ice, which is congealed with senseless cold,
>Should kindle fire by wonderful device?
Such is the power of love in gentle mind,
>That it can alter all the course of kind.   [kind-nature]

(4) *Songs*

The sonnet form has, as I said, a number of minor variants, in addition to the three main types I have just discussed. (Gerard Manley Hopkins even invented a "curtal" sonnet, a reduced-size form with ten and a fifth lines, structurally divided into two strophes, one of six and one of four and a fifth lines.) But the song has almost endless variations. Strictly, it is more readily definable by its tone than by its external characteristics (number of lines, rhyming pattern, and so on). Originally a poem meant to be sung, and often to be sung by the poet himself (Sir Thomas Wyatt was an expert lute player, and undoubtedly sang many of his own poems), "song" has gradually come to mean no more than a particularly lyric ("song-like") poem, something with unusually musical qualities. Some of the most delightful of all songs have been written for plays: Shakespeare is an extraordinary songwriter, too:

> Under the greenwood tree
> Who loves to lie with me,
> And turn his merry note   [turn-return]
> Unto the sweet bird's throat,
> Come hither, come hither, come hither!
> Here shall he see
> No enemy
> But winter and rough weather.
>
> (*As You Like It*)

> When icicles hang by the wall,
> And Dick the shepherd
>   blows his nail,   [i.e., blows on his cold hands]
> And Tom bears logs into the hall,
> And milk comes frozen home in pail,
> When blood is nipped,   [nipped-hurt by cold;
>   and ways be foul,   ways-roads, paths]
> Then nightly sings the staring owl:
> "Tu-who!
> Tu-whit, tu-who!" a merry note,
> While greasy Joan doth keel the pot.   [keel-stir]
>
> (*Love's Labours Lost*)

> Take, O, take those lips away
> That so sweetly were forsworn;
> And those eyes, the break of day,
> Lights that do mislead the morn;

But my kisses bring again, bring again;
Seals of love, but sealed in vain, sealed in vain.
                                    (*Measure for Measure*)

These three poems seem to me virtually a definition of
"lyric": their descriptions are exceedingly particular and
precise, but their meaning is far more implicit than it is
explicit. What is the precise point of the second poem
(strictly, the first half of the poem, since I have omitted
the second stanza, here)? Certain things happen in winter;
they are all described; the general effect is to evoke the
spirit of winter, to recreate it in a reader's (or a listener's)
mind. And that general effect *is* the point. The first poem is
a bit more pointed, saying that it is pleasant "under the
greenwood tree," and that the singer would welcome com-
pany in his bucolic delight. But poetry usually *says* more
than this. (It need not, but it usually does.) The third
Shakespeare song speaks sadly of a wonderful love, lost
and mourned for; it expresses the wonderfulness and the
sadness—and that, once more, is the poem's point. That is,
an archetypal song intends to express emotion in relatively
pure and highly musical language, and that expression of
emotion is its basic and often its sole purpose.

Certain structural and formal characteristics do tend to
recur, in songs, though there is no guaranteeing how a
particular poet will choose to shape a particular song.
Rhyme is fairly standard, even today. Tin-pan alley songs
(Cole Porter, Irving Berlin) always rhyme; Rock songs
(The Beatles, The Rolling Stones) rhyme much more
often than not; operatic songs (called "arias") almost always rhyme. That is, songs which are unmistakably intended for singing, as many poem-songs are not, any
longer (Shakespeare's of course were), nevertheless use
rhyme virtually all the time. It is clearly a musical feature,
a sound-decoration, which enhances the musical quality.
(It also tends to make songs easier to remember, which
was at one time—before printing, and relatively cheap
book-production—much more important than it is today.)

Irregular line-lengths are also a common feature. The
music of a poem proper tends to be a steady, regular
thing—though this is by no means a rule. The sonnet, for
example, is almost exclusively written in iambic pentameter,
all fourteen lines the same. (There have been hexameter
sonnets, tetrameter sonnets, even free verse sonnets.) Even
ballads and hymns tend to have regular metrical patterns,
though they too are oral forms. But the music—and I mean,

here, literally the music, the tune, the melody—of a song
requires that the words stretch this way and that. Melodies
which follow regular, predictable patterns do well enough
in folk songs (ballads, for example), where the music does
not have to fascinate, to capture attention and hold interest
as it does in the theater or on the concert stage. For the
composer to achieve rhythmical variety in the face of the
poetry is possible, but difficult; it makes better sense for
the poetry to not only permit, but actively to encourage this
variety in the music. Shakespeare obviously knew this,
whether or not he also wrote his own music (or shaped his
songs to pre-existing music: no one really knows). In some
of Wyatt's songs, indeed, it is only the necessity for suiting
words to music that can explain their odd form:

> And wilt thou leave me thus?
> Say nay, say nay, for shame,
> To save thee from the blame
> Of all my grief and grame;   [grame-sorrow]
> And wilt thou leave me thus?
> Say nay, say nay!

The repetitions of "say nay"—which are continued
throughout the rest of the poem—have almost no possible
justification outside the requirements of the melody. They
do not read badly, as poetry, but they do read rather me-
chanically. After a certain number of repetitions—there are
five instances of "say nay, say nay" in the complete poem—
the reader is likely to grow a bit weary of what seems, as
poetry, pretty much mindless. Of course, the musical
quality of the whole poem—and here I am, once again,
referring to verbal music—helps to make these repetitions
at least appropriate, expected. I am not criticizing Wyatt,
who is one of my personal favorites. I am trying only to
explain what he has done, and why he seems to have done
it.

Seventeenth-century songwriters did not much vary the
form, on the whole, though John Donne's songs might be
rather difficult to sing and Milton's, too, have a greater
density of language, a greater complexity of syntax than
the remarkable simplicity and purity displayed in Shakespeare's songs. The eighteenth century largely ignored the
form; the nineteenth employed it, but in mostly literary
rather than more strictly musical ways. A typical "Song"
by George Meredith, for example, is apt to begin:

> Love within the lover's breast
> Burns like Hesper in the west,

> O'er the ashes of the sun,
> Till the day and night are done;
> Then when dawn drives up her car—
> Lo! it is the morning star.

Whatever else one may say of it, this is pretty clearly not meant to be sung. Swinburne's "A Song in Time of Order" begins:

> Push hard across the sand,
>   For the salt wind gathers breath;
> Shoulder and wrist and hand,
>   Push hard as the push of death.

This is much more song-like; it still does not seem quite first-rate material for a composer to work with. Even so fine a lyric poet as John Keats is literary far more than musical, though the song which follows was, as he himself explained, written "to some Music as it was playing":

> I had a dove and the sweet dove died;
>   And I have thought it died of grieving;
> O, what could it grieve for? Its feet were tied,
>   With a silken thread of my own hand's weaving;
> Sweet little red feet! why should you die—
> Why should you leave me, sweet bird! why?
> You lived alone in the forest-tree,
> Why, pretty thing! would you not live with me?
> I kissed you oft and gave you white peas;
> Why not live sweetly, as in the green trees?

As poetry, bluntly, this is embarrassing—but for all that, I can imagine one of Keats' composer contemporaries, Schubert perhaps, setting this most readily to music. A few nineteenth-century poets did write what might be called true songs, still readable as poetry. Christina Rossetti, for example:

> When I am dead, my dearest,
>   Sing no sad songs for me;
> Plant thou no roses at my head,
>   Nor shady cypress tree . . .

It is still a bit literary (and sentimental), even a bit stiff, but clearly it can be sung.

Our own century's poets do not often write songs for singing. W. H. Auden begins his "Song for the New Year" (1937):

> It's farewell to the drawing-room's civilised cry
> The professor's sensible whereto and why . . .

Just try to sing that! And T. S. Eliot's "A Song for Simeon"
is rather less singable, beginning:

> Lord, the Roman hyacinths are blooming in bowls and
> The winter sun creeps by the snow hills . . .

Obviously, the word "song" has mutated: today's poets
simply do not mean the same thing by it as Shakespeare
did. I doubt that there is any unanimity, in fact, but my
impression is that, today, "song" means something like
"poem," and not much more than that. (There will be a
poem called "Sheep-Song," in my third collection. It begins:
"Sheep muddling in my mind/ Graze in the dark, feet flat,/
Teeth sawing roots/ And bark, lapping dried juice." It
could as logically be called "Sheep-Poem.") There *are*
some contemporary exceptions, however, notably in the
work of E. E. Cummings. He is capable of a "Song" of
deep musicality:

> Thy fingers make early flowers of
> all things . . .

A composer's hands might well begin to itch, coming on
such lines: they seem to me almost to demand musical
setting. But in this as in much else, Cummings bucked
the tide of his time. We are not a melodic age, either in
poetry or in music—which is not to say that song is dead,
or that we do not have other virtues.

(5) *Dialogues and Monologues*

I could, I suppose, have called this section something
like "Shorter dramatic forms." As soon as there are more
than two speakers, really, what we have is a play, not a
dramatic poem, and true drama, stage drama, is outside
the scope of this book. But with two speakers (a dialogue)
and a single speaker (a monologue) we are still in the
strictly literary form. Again, as with the song, just discussed, neither monologues nor dialogues have any set
structural pattern, nor any set rhyming pattern. The form
takes its basic definition from its dramatic character. The
Shakespearian soliloquies are monologues, but monologues
set in play-form; novels have a good deal of dialogue,
usually, but once again set in the novel-form. My concern
here is with poems, not with monologues and dialogues
which are part of other forms.

Robert Browning is both the best and the logical starting place. There had been poets writing dialogues and monologues, before him, but he is I think as much the father of the form as Wyatt is of the sonnet. Browning's viciously jealous monk is wonderfully convincing:

> Gr-r-r—there go, my heart's abhorrence!
>   Water your damned flower-pots, do!
> If hate killed men, Brother Lawrence,
>   God's blood, would not mine kill you?

The spluttering, hateful, impotent ending of the poem ("Soliloquy of the Spanish Cloister") is a marvel:

> Blasted lay that rose-acacia
>   We're so proud of! *Hy, Zy, Hine* . . .
> 'St, there's Vespers! *Plena gratia*
>   *Ave, Virgo!* Gr-r-r—you swine!

Browning even gives us—importantly, as I will show in a moment—a touch of the hated Brother Lawrence himself:

> . . . I must hear
> Wise talk of the kind of weather,
>   Sort of season, time of year:
> *Not a plenteous cork-crop: scarcely*
>   *Dare we hope oak-galls,*   [galls-plant fungi, etc.]
>   *I doubt:*
> *What's the Latin name for "parsley"?*
> What's the Greek name for Swine's Snout?

The poem is technically brilliant—musical, tightly balanced, with deft contrasts, as precise as it could be, tautly controlled, and completely clear. (With a little foot-noting, that is, to account for changes in culture, over the past hundred years.) And yet what makes it alive, makes it worth reading, is the subtlety of its dramatic portraits. This is not nearly so tangible a matter as precision or balance. The poem has often been talked of as a self-damning portrayal of the half-demented monk-speaker; it is sometimes assumed that his hatred for Brother Lawrence, which is clearly pathological, is also baseless. Good old Brother Lawrence, however, is also presented unfavorably. He is not a monster, to be sure, but he is clearly a terrible bore, and something of a prig—and in the close quarters of a monastery, he would be a difficult man to get on with, a man likely to bring out the worst, as he evidently has, in a weak and frustrated fellow monastic. Browning's monologue, in short, has real drama, and therefore has real merit, because it is psychologically true, it is not a cardboard mustering of ready-made types and pat generalizations. These are real people, still very real today: human psychology has not changed, essentially, since the beginning of recorded time. (If it had, could we still read Homer? Could we still read the Bible, much of which is older even than Homer?)

This is not an easy form. Poets fall, all too easily, into invented drama, and glue-pot psychology, when they try to make dramatic capital of another man's mind and spirit (another man real or imaginary). Walter Savage Landor's *Imaginary Conversations*, a long series of dialogues, works brilliantly—but these are dialogues written, not in poetry, but in prose. When Landor tried the poetic form that Browning later developed, he became stagey and melodramatic: the stuff simply does not ring true, and is neither read, now, nor readable. And the fact that it is a difficult, even a tricky form to handle, means that not many poets can possibly make of it, as Browning did, a regular feature of their work. T. S. Eliot wrote some fine monologues, early in his career; Robert Frost, too, wrote some excellent dialogues ("The Death of the Hired Man," "Two Witches"). Ezra Pound, too, has used the form extremely well, though he strains at it a bit, making his scenes a touch too dramatic, a whiff stagey. His "Sestina: Altaforte," for example, begins:

> Damn it all! All this our South stinks peace.
> You whoreson dog, Papiols, come!

This has great energy, and a considerable vividness—but the sound-level is turned just too high for credibility to be complete. One cannot quite hear the poetry, or feel the psychology, for the noise involved. Even Browning's principal twentieth-century heir, Edward Arlington Robinson, who wrote some of the most popular and influential of dramatic monologues (as well as many exceedingly popular dramatic lyrics—"Richard Cory," "Miniver Cheevy," "Luke Havergal"), began with fake drama:

> And now, my brother, it is time
> For me to tell the truth to you!
> To tell the story of a crime
> As black as Mona's eyes were blue.—
> Yes, here to-night, before I die . . .

This is the opening of "For Calderon," and one gets the feeling that Robinson tried to cram everything he could into the poem, making extravagant claims for its drama which, in the end, he could not (and does not) justify. The poem is sentimental, untrue, and of strictly historical interest. But Robinson went on to write "Mr. Flood's Party" and "Ben Jonson Entertains a Man From Stratford," and he can be forgiven.

The form's current status remains one of great popularity, especially among second- and third-rate poets, but of no very great achievement. The total number of successful monologues and dialogues is, in short, not large, nor is it growing very fast. There are exceptions—and they show, like David Wevill's fine monologue, "Caspar Hauser," that when a good poet honestly feels what he is writing about, there need be no staginess, no strain:

> Came to the Nurenberg gate,
> The second day of Pentecost,
> Staggering voiceless against walls in the dark—
> Able to see in the dark, seeing
> As I'd spent all my life in the dark of that stable
> Alone . . .

The spare, taut writing, here, shows too that the resources of contemporary poetry are available for the form. Good poets can still turn to it, as Browning and E. A. Robinson did. If they want to.

But they don't, and if you turn the pages of slim books of poetry, and come upon one monologue and dialogue after another, keep these warnings in mind.

(6) *Narratives*

This section will not deal with book-length narratives, whether the full epic (Homer's *The Iliad*, *The Odyssey*, Milton's *Paradise Lost*), the philosophical excursion (Dante's *The Divine Comedy*, Wordsworth's *The Prelude*), or the quasi-drama (Goethe's *Faust*). These are much more like novels, in important ways, and to a considerable extent they call for a kind of analysis that has not been broached, in this book. There is no question, of course, that these book-length poems are poems. Much that has been said here is plainly relevant to them, as well as to the shorter works which *have* been discussed. Separating these long poems out is therefore arbitrary, to some degree, but in a small book there isn't room to tackle the large issues raised by such large forms. I would rather omit them than treat them with inevitable superficiality.

Shorter narrative poems are not, in comparison to these

larger poetic narratives, simply of lesser length. Longer works move partly into the world of *fiction;* shorter narrative poems stay far more in the orbit of all other, non-narrative *poems.* In the shorter span, that is, the weight and significance of the poetry itself is greater than it can be over the longer distance. The poet is more aware, too, of writing poetry than of writing a story—or, to put it a bit differently, he is less likely to forget that he is writing a poem. And the kinds of literary devices he will use are different, too: the texture of his poem will be richer, and its dependence on (or ability to make use of) such non-verbal structuring as plot and subplot, flash-backs, jumps in space and time, will necessarily be lessened. In *Hamlet,* for example, Shakespeare can afford to follow all sorts of minor trails—Rosencrantz and Guildenstern, the strolling players, the plight of Ophelia, the fate of Polonius, even the character of Fortinbras. In his narrative poem, *Venus and Adonis,* however, Shakespeare has almost 1,200 lines of verse but concentrates quite remarkably on the scorned goddess and the scorning mortal. *Hamlet* can afford to begin without the prince on stage, but *Venus and Adonis* begins, from the first line, to describe the setting for the central incident, Adonis' destruction by the wild boar he has been hunting.

> Even as the sun with purple-colored face
> Had ta'en his last leave of the weeping morn,
> Rose-cheeked Adonis hied him to   [hied him-hurried]
>   the chase.
> Hunting he loved, but love he laughed to scorn.

In his *The Rape of Lucrece,* Shakespeare used almost 1,900 lines—very close to the length of *Sir Gawain and the Green Knight,* and better than half the length of *Beowulf*—but still sticks remarkably close to his main figures and to the one chief incident he is concerned with. Lucrece's husband and father, and a few of her husband's friends, make brief entrances; for most of its length the poem focuses only on Tarquin, the rapist, and Lucrece, whom he rapes. Even after Collatine, Lucrece's husband, makes his appearance, after the rape, he is there largely for her to speak to him, for her to explain, to accuse, and to die.

The narrative poem, then, tends to focus more on incident than on the complex narrative found in the novel. It also tends to focus more on verbal texture than does the novel (or than do novel-like forms): there is much more decoration, much more lingering over descriptions, much more permissiveness about such verbal structuring as philosophical or mythological digressions. Christopher Marlowe's *Hero and Leander,* for example—a poem about the beautiful Hero and her lover Leander, who swam the Hellespont to be with her and afterwards was drowned swimming home—spends its first four lines talking about the physical setting of the narrative, then takes forty-six lines to describe the beauties of beautiful Hero. To describe, but not to analyze her—for this is not a poetic monologue or dialogue, in which the emphasis would be on characterization. Hero is she "whom young Apollo courted for her hair." We are told of the "purple silk" with which her clothes are lined, the "chains of pebble stone" she wore "about her neck," and that "she wore no gloves, for neither sun nor wind/ Would burn or parch her hands." Similarly, Leander has "dangling tresses that were never shorn . . . His body was as straight as Circe's wand,/ Jove might have sipped out nectar from his hand." What went on in Leander's head, other than desire for Hero, is hard to know; if Hero herself had an idea or a concern other than Leander, we are not told of it.

The decorative tendency is less strong, though still clear, in Milton; it is less strong, as well, in Dryden, whose fine *Absalom and Achitophel* (1681) is heavily Milton-influenced. But by the nineteenth century, narrative poetry is again verbally expansive, centered on incident rather than on full-scale plot, and distinctly more decorative than fictional or experiential. The glory of nineteenth-century narrative, to my mind, is Byron's fabulous *Don Juan* (pronounced "jew-un"):

> I want a hero: an uncommon want,
>   When every year and month sends forth a new one,
> Till, after cloying the gazettes with cant,
>   The age discovers he is not the true one;
> Of such as these I should not care to vaunt,
>   I'll therefore take our ancient friend Don Juan—
> We all have seen him, in the pantomime,
> Sent to the devil somewhat ere his time.
>
> Most epic poets plunge
>   'in medias res'   [i.e., in the middle of things]
>   (Horace makes this the heroic turnpike road),
> And then your hero tells, whene'er you please,
>   What went before—by way of episode,
> While seated after dinner at his ease,
>   Beside his mistress in some soft abode,

> Palace, or garden, paradise, or cavern,
> Which serves the happy couple for a tavern.

It's a rollicking, sometimes serious, always delightful poem, incident piled on incident; it is even less like an orthodox novel than such unorthodox novels as *Tristram Shandy* or *Don Quixote*, both of which it slightly resembles. Byron did not live to finish it: never mind, it could not really have an ending, or enough narrative shape to even require an ending.

Keats too, in his fanciful and yet powerful adaptation of a grisly Boccaccio tale, "Isabella, or The Pot of Basil," subordinates character and plot to delineation of mood and incident. The dead beloved, Lorenzo, takes on more reality, as a decapitated head buried in a pot of basil, than he ever has as a living man; Isabella's two murderous brothers are stock villains; Isabella herself is a succession of states of mind, first gay intoxication, then misery, then morbidity and madness. Mood is virtually everything—and is extraordinarily well done. Anyone who reads Keats' *Endymion,* described by the poet as a "romance," for its plot, is surely mad. But it is beautiful poetry, for all that:

> A thing of beauty is a joy for ever:
> Its loveliness increases; it will never
> Pass into nothingness; but still will keep
> A bower quiet for us, and a sleep
> Full of sweet dreams, and health, and quiet breathing.

And Keats' lovely tale, "The Eve of St. Agnes" ("St. Agnes' Eve—Ah, bitter chill it was!"), is similarly built on incident and mood. The detail is often sharp, precise, real, but detail is not the same thing as plot.

Think of Coleridge's "The Rime of the Ancient Mariner," purportedly a story-poem and clearly a narrative in at least the sense used in this section. Mood, incident: this is what the poem is all about, "a painted ship/ Upon a painted ocean." We know absolutely nothing about the transfixed wedding guest, who hears the whole tale from the weird old Mariner, except that when the tale was done,

> He went like one that hath been stunned,
> And is of sense forlorn:
> A sadder and a wiser man,
> He rose the morrow morn.

It is basically a question of emphasis. I have not been saying that poems like "The Rime of the Ancient Mariner" are not "true" narratives (whatever that might mean), or that they do not tell a story. They do, and usually a good story, a story impossible to break away from. But they tell their stories differently, they stress other things than plain narration. They are, as I said earlier, more poem than plot—and perhaps it is just as well to leave it at that.

(7) *Discursive free forms*

This sounds like a rag-bag heading, and it is. How else, though, am I to describe all the variant forms used by contemporary poets, especially—forms which vary every known component of the more traditional ways of putting poems together.

> Underneath the tree on some
> soft grass I sat, I
>
> watched two happy
> woodpeckers be dis-
>
> turbed by my presence. And
> why not, I thought to
>
> myself, why
> not.

This is Robert Creeley's fine "Like They Say"—and what is the form? Creeley makes very sure that it cannot be taken as a poem built on a couplet base: he not only heavily enjambs (runs over) every single line, and most especially each even-numbered line (except of course the last), but he even splits up a word, "dis-/ turbed," as though to emphasize the nontraditional, noncouplet nature of what he is up to. There is some metrical structuring— the poem winds down with fewer stresses per line, at the end—but not a very great deal. There is no rhyme. There *is* plenty of reason, but it is not the same rationality we find in the sonnet. Creeley writes, as indeed he obviously thinks and feels, by a standard which makes the old categorizations not quite relevant. There has not been enough time for these new approaches to form to become, if ever they do, standardized, to acquire names and labels—and so I shall here call such untraditional forms "discursive free forms," for lack of anything better to call them.

They can be very effectively deployed (and very ingeniously, and very complexly, and sometimes too they can be very difficult to follow):

Why have they stripped the grass from the sides of the road,
leaving the worms agape, and a senseless load
of brick-ends and broken glass? Tomorrow it will
start to show again. For this is what it means.

One thinks of those critics for whom the outside is
    a dreadful bore:
they scrape for the ambiguous, dig for the profound, deep,
    deep beneath the ground—
what you read on the surface of the agitated page is
    only an idle dusty weed.

This is the beginning of "The Interpreters (or, How to Bury
Yourself in a Book)," by D. J. Enright. It begins as though
traditional forms are to be observed: lines one and two
are a rhymed iambic pentameter couplet. The meter begins
to falter (or alter, depending on your point of view) in
line three. Line four cannot possibly be read as iambic
pentameter and, unlike line two, it does not rhyme with
the line before it. If then the first two lines are clearly a
couplet, the next two lines are clearly something different.
But what? Lines five, six, and seven (and indeed the rest
of this almost forty-line poem) are neither iambic nor
pentameter, they do not rhyme, there is no possibility of
a couplet in this kind of three-line strophe—and, in short,
whatever the form is, it is determining its own structure,
and evolving, changing as it works through the thing that
this particular poet, at this particular time, wants to say.

There is no necessary anarchy in this. Other, nonverbal
arts have long since crossed this Rubicon. If a composer
writes a symphony, today—and most do not—it is not
likely to be a symphony in classical form: four movements,
allegro, andante, minuet (or scherzo), and allegro, with
the first allegro having two subjects, two developments, and
a recapitulation—etc. (Camille Saint-Saëns' only comment
on the Franck D Minor Symphony, at its première per-
formance, is said to have been: "The English horn does
not solo." What would he save said—what *did* he say,
since he lived a very long time—to Stravinsky?) Prokofiev
did write a miniature "classical symphony," but largely to
convince hostile critics that, although he preferred to write,
for example, a scherzo for sixteen bassoons, he could also
write in the old ways if he chose to. If he chose not to,
that is, it was not out of either ignorance or incompetence.
Painters, too, are no longer turning out "Still Life, with
Candles and a Pear," or "My Father at Dawn, Reading
the Manchester Weekly Without Glasses." Anyone who

thinks—as some people still do—that Vincent Van Gogh painted as he did because he did not know any better, should study Van Gogh's early sketches and drawings, in which traditional draughtsmanship is beautifully handled. And was Frank Lloyd Wright to design wigwams? or igloos? another Parthenon, another Sistine Chapel?

It is not contempt for form which makes contemporary artists break old molds, but precisely love of form. The old forms (like old clothes) were developed out of life in another world, with different needs and different ways of expressing them. As people change, styles change—in everything. Art is, as I've said over and over, very much a part of our world, and so, inevitably, it changes too. The artist who paints like Rembrandt, today, is either no artist, or a fake, or quite simply mad. We can learn from Rembrandt, but we cannot learn to be him, in his world, in his time, living and thinking and doing everything a man does in the course of a day, things little and things large. Artists love form; some are better at controlling it, at mastering it, than others, but all love to handle it. This is a good part of being what an artist must be. And if social codes are breaking down, if national codes are breaking down, why should we expect that artistic (or any other) codes will be immune from the process of mutation? Would it be a good thing, indeed, to have the moral code of, say, the year 70 in the year 1970? The question is ridiculous. What then makes the moral code of 1870 any more absolute and imperishable? Or the artistic code?

Another way of looking at the newer forms of newer poetry is this: conscious of form, devoted to form, but aware that everything in his world is shifting and cracking, the poet is now put in the position of having constantly to *re-invent* form. A form may be both new and brilliant, but it is less likely, today, than ever before, to be used over and over. And even less likely than that to be used by anyone other than its inventor. The fine stanza invented by John Berryman for his extraordinary *Dream Songs* is distinctly and entirely personal to John Berryman. Indeed, a form may be invented (or re-invented) for a single use—like my own "Interfaith Dialogue," in which the formal principle is that each line has one more stress than the one before it (except that lines five and six stick at five stresses apiece), building to the seven-stress penultimate (next-to-last) line, followed by the very short final line:

Not words
But verbal process
Of high ingenuity and taste
Leading to monographs, lectures, tours
Of gravestones, glossy books of prints, piles
Of reports, banquets, committees of scholars with
    a world
To create but neither glue nor gum nor paste
    from which
To accumulate anything but verbal process of high
    ingenuity and taste
And other committees.

I have never again used this form, nor do I think I am likely to—though in another poem in the same book, a poem called "Buffalo, 1967," there are a total of five strophes, the first having five lines, the second having four lines, and so on, down to the one-line final stanza. This sort of thing is anything but a lack of interest in form. It is, rather, a creative interest in form; it makes for an external newness which the reader can, I know, find disconcerting. We all like the familiar better than the new—but in the end the *best* turns out to be better still, if we can overcome our perfectly natural reluctance to deal with the new. We need to try.

CHAPTER FIVE: Metrics and History

Metrics is not a subject for the layman. Only a poet really understands it, in my opinion, and most poets do not like to discuss what is as much a part of their being as absolute pitch is to some composers. Have you ever tried to get someone to *explain* absolute pitch, someone who had it? I do not have it, and I have tried to get it explained to me—and the result is inarticulate hash. (So too are, in my view, virtually all discussions of metrics by nonpoets—some of whom have the gall to term themselves "metricists"!)

What I want to do, in this chapter, is to discuss metrics in context, which means in history. To discuss it abstractly seems to me almost worthless: even poets cannot easily retain the various forbidding names for the various metrics —and I for one have looked up the word "oxymoron" thirty or forty times. As I write this, I do not have the faintest notion of what "oxymoron" means. Nor frankly do I much care: it is the *thing* which interests me, the poetry and its processes, not the rather artificial labels and rules which nonpoets have erected, like a fence, to keep nonexperts out. I cannot, in one brief chapter, write a connected history of English metrics, nor do I want to. My goal is an examination of the metrical practices of a few leading poets, from Chaucer's time down to our own, so that you can perhaps develop some feeling for what poets do and why (and when) they do it. This seems to me more likely to be of genuine help, and also more likely to stay with you.

Chaucer did not invent iambic pentameter, but he might just as well have. It was his example, his practice, which established that metric as the base on which, for centuries, all English poetry was created. The pronunciation of Middle English (that is, the form of English spoken from roughly 1100 to roughly 1500) is not really difficult; it seems much harder than in fact it is. You need, of course, to understand the *sound* of verse before you can understand its movement. (It is an excellent rule to always read a poem aloud: your voice can be your own best teacher.)

> A knyght there was, and that a worthy man,
> That fro the tyme that he first began   [fro-from]
> To riden out, he loved chivalrie,
> Trowth and honour, fredom   [trowth-truth]
>   and courtesie.

In rough approximation, and with stresses indicated by capital letters, here is how this sounds (and note, please, that every letter, every syllable, is meant to be sounded):

> a KNICHT there WAHSS, ahnd THAT a WAHRthy MAHN,
> that FROW the TEEM-uh THAT hay FEHRST beGAHN
> tow REED-en OHT, hay LOW-ved SHIV-al-REE-uh,
> TROWTH ahnd AHN-oor, FRAY-dom ahnd KOOR-ta-SEE-uh.

This is—though you may at first have to read it several times before your tongue becomes supple enough to let you hear it—a very flexible, musical iambic pentameter. It is basically regular, although the third and fourth lines end with a feminine rhyme (that is, having an extra unstressed syllable), and the fourth line begins with what is called a "beheaded iamb" (that is, an iamb without its front or unstressed half); after its third stress, the fourth line also has two unstressed syllables instead of the usual one. But these irregularities are the farthest thing from errors or faults: every good poet writes according to the music of the words, not according to the prescription of some metrical convention. Where there is a metrical convention, and the poet chooses to adhere to it, he does not adhere to it slavishly—and this is not just a question of regularity, of choosing not to obey the traffic rules. *Knyght,* in the first line, above, is a stressed word, and so is *was,* but no one with any kind of ear, no one with any feeling for the music of the English language, will put as much stress on *was,* here, as he will on *knyght.* Further: the first word in the line, *a,* is unstressed, and it is followed by a stressed word, *knyght:* this is of course what iambic verse is all about, the alternation of unstressed and stressed syllables. But in the next foot (that is, the next complete iambic sequence: each complete sequence in a particular metrical pattern is known as a "foot"), the unstressed syllable is the word *there* and the stressed syllable is the word *was*—but there is not a very great difference between them. And *there,* clearly, has more stress than does the word *a,* just two words before it in the line. What matters, then, is the relationship between the syllables within a particular foot: whichever of them is more heavily stressed is considered, for that foot, *the* stressed syllable, and whichever of them is less heavily stressed is considered, for that foot, the unstressed syllable. Note that I have said "is considered": these things are plainly relative and, in the narrow sense of the word, "conventional" (that is, agreed upon). The fàct that the word *there,* for example, is considered to be unstressed, because of its position vis-à-vis the word *was,* cannot take away the comparatively greater stress on *there,* vis-à-vis, *a,* which is inherent in their relative standing in the English language. In the language, mind you, quite apart from this line of poetry, *there* is literally weightier than *a,* and no metrical convention can either undo or ignore that fact.

But metrical conventions do *not*—as poets in fact practice them—ignore these linguistic realities. Rather, the metrical conventions exploit them, play on them and with them. In this brief Chaucerian passage, as I have marked it for you, you must not read like a steam pile-driver, every unstressed syllable light and soft—equally light and soft— and every stressed syllable loud and heavy—equally loud and heavy. No poet writes that kind of verse; no one who reads poetry at all well reads it that way. Rather, let the lines take their natural linguistic shape, let the stresses fall where they would if this were ordinary speech, or prose, not Poetry. And then, where a metrical convention is being used, and you happen to know what it is, give some consideration to how the poet meant to have the linguistic facts fit into the metrical patterns. Because that *is* what he wants: no poet writes in the face of linguistic fact, no poet has ever felt that metrical convention was superior to the reality of his language. In Richard Wagner's opera *Die Meistersinger,* The Mastersingers, which is written about a guild of poets and songwriters, the goat of the story, one Sextus Beckmesser (modelled, incidentally, on a music critic Wagner particularly disliked, Eduard Hanslick), is constantly trying to force both words and music into cramped, unnatural patterns, without regard either to their rhythm or even to their sense. In his final, ludicrous scene, Beckmesser so slops up a stolen song that he is hooted into silence. The letter without the spirit, Wagner is saying, is laughable and, worse still, impotent. Art by

the book is not art, but parody. Poems are not written by
rules, but by men.

The pacifist, Mohandas Gandhi, recruited for the
British army in World War I. The best thing is to be a
pacifist and not fight, he said. The worst thing is to be a
coward and run away from a fight. If you can't be a
pacifist, it is better to fight than be a coward. In reading
poetry, it is better if you understand the convention by
which the poet was guided, and can therefore read his
lines with just about the same rhythm he meant them to
have. But I would rather have poetry read to a natural
rhythm, and read "wrongly" (that is, not as it was intended to be read), than read rigidly and artificially, but
according to the letter of the convention.

Four lines of Chaucer are not enough to sense very
much of his metrical flavor. Here are several more passages; all of these examples are from his *Canterbury Tales:*

> There was also a Nun, a prioresse,
> That of hir smiling was full   [hir-her;
>   simple and coy;   coy-quiet]
> Hir greatest oath was but by Saint Loy;
> And she was cleped Madame Eglentyne. [cleped-called]
> Full well she sung the sérvicé divíne,
> Entúned ín hir nóse full sémelý,   [semely-pleasing]
> And Frenssh she spak full fair   [spak-spoke;
>   and fetisly.   fetisly-neatly]
> After the schol of Stratford atte Bowe.

> And Í seyde hís opínión was góod.   [seyde-said]
> What sholde he study and make   [what-why;
>   himselven wood,   wood-crazy]
> Upon a book in cloister alwáys to pour,
> Or swinken with his handes, ánd labóure, [swinken-work]
> As Austyn bit? How   [Austyn-St. Augustine; bit-ordered]
>   shall the world be served?
> Let Austyn have his swink to him reserved!

(I have marked some of the odder stresses with stress
signs. The word LABOR, for example, has a distinctly French
sound, in Chaucer's English—and indeed it was freshly
borrowed into English.)

Chaucer's music stresses motion. It is completely and
elegantly precise; balance is one of its chief points. It tends
to be light in texture: Chaucer's vocabulary does not draw
its foreign-language borrowings from Latin, as Shakespeare's does, but from the lighter-textured French, nor

does Chaucer load his lines down with adjectives of any kind, let alone portentous ones. There are only nine adjectives in these three passages taken together, and they are: *worthy, first, simple, coy* (quiet), *greatest, divine, good, wood* (crazy), and *reserved*. This is a remarkably unadorned list—nor does Chaucer much change his practice when the poem is intensely, darkly serious, like much of his great romance (and one of my favorite long poems in the world), *Troilus and Criseyde*:

> A nyghtyngale, upon a cedar grene,   [grene-green]
> Under the chambre wall there as she lay,
> Full loude sung ayein the moone   [ayein-against]
>   shene,
> Peraunter, in his   [peraunter-perhaps; briddes-
>   briddes wise, a lay   bird's; wise-way; lay-song]
> Of love, that made hire hearte fressh
>   and gay.

There are four adjectives, here: *grene, loude, fressh,* and *gay.* The point is not simply that Chaucer's vocabulary is "fressh and gay," but that, inevitably, the weight of the words you read, in poetry, helps determine the weight, the speed, and the texture of that poetry. Prosody (another word for metrics) is *not* a mechanical art, the cold study of fixed meters and frozen phonetics. It is a living art, dealing with a living phenomenon—language. Without the life, there is no art—and of course no metrics, either!

The light texture, and the rather quick motion, of Chaucer's poetry is expressed in a variety of ways. Only one of the four brief passages I have quoted does not contain an enjambed (run-over) line, and that is the gently satiric description of the "prioresse." It is still uncertain—there has been a good deal of debate—whether "entuned in hir nose full semely" is meant to be quietly comic, or whether it is merely descriptive of a particular style of ecclesiastical singing. But there is no doubt that the praise given the lady's ability to speak French, "full fair and fetisly," is delicately qualified by the information, immediately following, that this is not the French of Paris, but "after the schol of Stratford atte Bowe." In this passage, Chaucer anticipates the heroic (end-stopped) couplets of Dryden and Pope, which were of course very often used for satiric purposes. But in the other satirical passage I have quoted, that about the monk who does not want to stay in his cloister and study holy books, "or swinken with his handes, and laboure," Chaucer uses a line of great

energy, in fact aping the fierce determination of the worldly
monk to defend his "religious" stance. It is a masterful
aping, subtle and deadly accurate—and much of its force
depends on this capturing of the swaggering roll of the
monk's own speech.

Chaucer's musical arsenal is well enough stocked, indeed, to catch any rhythm he wants: if he does not use a
particular verbal movement, it is because he does not
choose to, and not because he is unable to. (Similarly, he
can and usually does rhyme closely, but sometimes the
kind of imperfect rhyme of semely/fetisly seems to him
preferable, and he does not hesitate to adapt his principles
to his practice. —The point is, of course, that good poets
have much more practice than they do principle. They
tend to theorize with pen in hand, not out of context and
abstractly.)

There are some unique characteristics of Chaucer's
prosody, namely the now-vanished sounds of Middle English. The vowels, in the passage I marked for you, above,
must seem very strange to the uninitiated ear—and I have
tried to mark only the most important things. The "th"
sound in "that," for example, is in fact unvoiced, not
voiced as it is today; that is, it is the "th" of "thin" rather
than the "th" of "this." The "r" sound is different, too,
more like the kind of rolled "r" that operatic singers sometimes use, in performing folk songs in English. The conso-
nants are sounded, often—as in "knyght," where the "k"
is always heard and the "gh" has a sound something like
the German "ch"—in words where modern English no
longer sounds them. The overall effect is inevitably unusual, to ears attuned only to contemporary English, and
this may make appreciation of Chaucer's music a bit
harder. When you come to know it well, it is a delightful
music, light, spare, quick, and as subtle and delicate as
a glass of good (French) champagne.

Shakespeare is another thing entirely. Writing roughly
two hundred years later, in a language much altered by
time, and in a society much altered by changed political
and economic conditions, as well as by modest growths in
technology, Shakespeare creates a more rounded, complex,
and deeper-toned verbal music. The breath-line is longer—
that is, pauses come fewer and farther between, and the
length of the individual rhythmic elements is much greater.
Enjambement, accordingly, is often not just a matter of a
run-over line, but of several run-on lines in a row:

> Angelo,
> There is a kind of character in thy life
> That to th' observer doth thy history
> Fully enfold. Thyself and thy belongings
> Are not thine own so proper as to waste
> Thyself upon thy virtues, they on thee.
>
> (*Measure for Measure*)

I think you can hear, at once, that this is a different voice than any in which Chaucer chooses to speak. It is not heavy: Shakespeare keep his long-breathed lines beautifully afloat, they do not sag. But if we can perhaps compare Chaucer to a musical tenor, then Shakespeare is a musical baritone—suave and full, but unmistakably deeper and rounded. The thought-line, too, is as much extended as is the breath-line: four lines down from the passage I have just quoted, Shakespeare has the Duke say:

> Spirits are not finely touched
> But to fine issues, nor Nature never lends
> The smallest scruple of her excellence
> But, like a thrifty goddess, she determines
> Herself the glory of a creditor,
> Both thanks and use.

In different terms, this is closer to oratory, to what we today loosely call rhetoric, than is almost anything in Chaucer.

There are other satisfactions in this music, of course, than there are in Chaucer's. Sustaining a long melodic line, through a series of deft and swift changes and pauses and variations, finally emerging with a logical and rounded-off harmonic resolution, is a very deep pleasure indeed, for the listener/reader. It is, let me emphasize, only different from Chaucer, and not either better or worse: when poets reach the level of Chaucer and Shakespeare it is almost idle to talk about degrees of excellence (though we do it, and I have done it, even in this book). The orchestration is necessarily different, too. Note the adjectives in these two passages: *proper, touched, fine, smallest, thrifty*. It is plainly a different sort of list, with more words expressive of moral concern, and without the bright, gay adjectives we found in Chaucer. Nor is even so early and frothy a play as *A Midsummer Night's Dream* much different:

> Things base and vile, holding no quantity,
> Love can transform to form and dignity.

> Love looks not with the eyes, but with the mind,
> And therefore is wing'd Cupid painted blind.

("Wing'd Cupid," which puts two stressed words in a row, is a common metrical variation, called a "spondee.")

The metrical patterns of Shakespeare's verse are about as regular, or as irregular, as Chaucer's—perhaps a bit freer, with a few more unstressed syllables, but on the whole not drastically altered. Shakespeare is still writing iambic pentameter, and in the early plays especially he rhymes quite freely. Even in *Hamlet,* indeed, the rhymed couplet, used as an exit line, occurs frequently:

> The play's the thing
> Wherein I'll catch the conscience of the King.

Or:

> It shall be so.
> Madness in great ones must not unwatched go.

Or:

> O, come away!
> My soul is full of discord and dismay.

But in general the use of rhyme drops off, in the later plays; the verse is still iambic pentameter, but in the form known as "blank verse" (which simply means that the iambic pentameter does not rhyme):

> Mother, for love of grace,
> Lay not that flattering unction to your soul,
> That not your trespass but my madness speaks.
>
> *(Hamlet)*

The requirements of complexity tend to push a poet away from rhyme. (John Milton came to hate rhyme so passionately that he called it "no necessary adjunct or true ornament of poem or good verse . . . but the invention of a barbarous Age, to set off wretched matter and lame meter.") The music of poetry, after all, is a carrier, and not that which is carried; it is more a tool than, usually, a thing in itself. To express more complex thoughts, the poet will often need to use more complex rhythms, and rhyme will make that more and more difficult. None of this is absolute: rhymed poetry can be just as complex as unrhymed poetry. But it is clearly (and quite naturally) harder to be complex and also to rhyme, and the human tendency, in both art and life, is to conserve one's energy as much as possible, to take an airplane from San Francisco to New York, rather than to walk.

Shakespeare's prosody is not exhausted by these brief comments. I have talked, in this book, about his songs, his sonnets, his narrative poems, and the poetry in his plays—but there is even more than this, for the plays contain poetry of many varieties, and also contain prose of many varieties too. Indeed, he can be virtually as clear and delicate as Chaucer, when he wants (or needs) to be:

> [Miranda:]   I do not know
> One of my sex; no woman's face remember,
> Save, from my glass, mine own; nor   [glass-mirror]
>   have I seen
> More that I may call men than you, good friend,
> And my dear father.
>
> (*The Tempest*)

Note, however, that the stresses are far more subdued, here, than in Chaucer, the music less obviously perceptible. Chaucer's English (he died in 1400) is itself a more rugged thing, with sharper contrasts; by Shakespeare's time (he died in 1616) the language had become more flowing, less strong, perhaps, but certainly smoother. This change in language cannot help but enforce a change in poetic music. It is not that Chaucer sticks more closely to the iambic pentameter convention than Shakespeare does. It is, rather, that both men follow the sounds and rhythms of the speech of their day; iambic metrics are natural to English, in every time from Chaucer's to our own, but the accentuation differs from one age to another. The lines spoken by Miranda, quoted above, are delicate in good part because they are spoken by a very young and singularly innocent girl, a girl who has, as she says, never seen another female and who has seen almost no men. The words are simple, most of them monosyllabic. The only adjectives are *good* and *dear*. And yet the long-breathed line remains: this is not, all other things aside, a passage that Chaucer is likely to have written, on rhythmic grounds alone.

The central facts of seventeenth-century verbal music can be established, I think, if we look—briefly—at Milton's verse. (It would be helpful to examine, also, the prosody of John Donne, and George Herbert, and Ben Jonson, and Robert Herrick—but this would be an endless chapter, if I did examine these poets as well.)

He scarce had ceased, when the superior fiend [i.e., Satan]
Was moving toward the shore; his ponderous shield
Ethereal temper, massy,   [ethereal temper-
    large and round,   celestially hard]
Behind him cast; the broad circumference
Hung on his shoulders like the moon, whose orb
Through optic glass the Tuscan   [Tuscan artist-Galileo]
    artist views
At evening from the top of Fesole,
Or in Valdarno, to descry new lands,
Rivers or mountains in her spotty globe.

This is as much knottier than Shakespeare as Shakespeare
is than Chaucer. To say that Milton's English is heavily
Latinized is to state the obvious: there is Latin in both
his vocabulary and his syntax. There are ten adjectives in
this passage, which is a far greater concentration than in
either Chaucer or Shakespeare—and the adjectives are of
a very different character: *superior, ponderous, ethereal,
massy, large, round, broad, optic, new,* and *spotty*. The
iambic pentameter is superficially about as regular as
Shakespeare's—not quite, because the fifth line begins with
a trochee (the reverse of an iamb: a stressed followed by
an unstressed syllable)—but in fact falls away from iambic
to a considerable degree, since the stresses do not easily
or naturally fall out as five to a line. I doubt that Milton
pronounced "circumference" with four syllables, rather
than three, but it must be sounded with four—and two
of them stressed—in order for the line to be iambic: be-
HIND him CAST; the BROAD circUMferENCE. Anything this
unnatural begins to seem unlikely; indeed, the great metrical
experimenter and poetic radical, Gerard Manley Hopkins,
claimed Milton as an early colleague in rhythmic revolution. In the fifth line, again, "like" must be stressed, to
make the iambic pentameter fit the prescribed pattern. The
next to last line similarly requires that either "or" or "in"
be stressed, and the final line needs a stress on "in"—all
of which is possible, but all of which taken together is a
bit much.

The passage is in fact violently eccentric, by earlier
metrical standards. More than half the lines are enjambed,
which is a singularly high percentage. Milton was passionately fond of Italian: he naturally wrote poems in
Latin and in Greek, as most educated men of his time
regularly did, but Milton wrote, also, in Italian, and wrote
fluently as well. And there is something distinctly Italianate

about this passage: read aloud, the vowels have an insistent open roundness which is much more Italianate, in fact, than it is English. It is neither heavy, exactly, nor thick: it is simply colored over with a patina (surface coloring) of foreign sounds, of un-English vowel effects. It is English, plainly: do not misunderstand me. It is English, and it is readily comprehensible as English—but it is unusual English, and the unusualness comes, in part, from the very high percentage of vowels, and among the vowels the very high percentage of open, round vowels (MOOVing TOHRd the SHOHr; his PAHNdrous SHEELD).

Later in the poem—the passage I have been discussing comes from Milton's great epic, *Paradise Lost*—Adam looks up and sees the angel Raphael descending to earth:

> "Haste hither, Eve, and worth thy sight behold
> Eastward among those trees, what glorious shape
> Comes this way moving; seems another morn
> Ris'n on mid-noon . . ."

The Italianate patina is not so strong, here, but the musical eccentricity remains. The first line opens with an iamb that is just barely iambic, is almost a spondee: the stress on "hither" is greater, but not much greater than the stress on "haste" (which must be considered, according to the metrical convention, an unstressed syllable). And the next three lines all begin with stressed syllables. Line two and line four are clearly trochaic, for the first foot: EASTward a-MONG . . . RIS'N on mid-NOON. . . . Line three is probably trochaic in its first foot, as well, but how much real difference in stress is there, here, among its first four words, "Comes this way moving"? One could easily make a small pause after the first word, "comes," and thereby stress each of these first four words—and also the fifth word, which comes after the pause (caesura) dictated by the semi-colon! The enjambement of this passage, further, is complete: each of the three complete lines is a run-over line.

A poet who experiments this much with iambic pentameter, who obviously feels a kind of decay already set into its fabric, can be expected to experiment with other meters—and Milton does. His "An Epitaph on the Marchioness of Winchester," apparently written in iambic tetrameter couplets (that is, couplets with four iambic feet, rather than five), is in fact written in an extraordinarily irregular metric, sometimes four feet (or stresses:

it is hard to know exactly what Milton had in mind, at times), sometimes three, and not always iambic, either:

> This rich marble doth inter
> The honoured wife of Winchester,
> A Viscount's daughter, an Earl's heir,
> Besides what her virtues fair
> Added to her noble birth,
> More than she could own from Earth.

That first line must be read with a spondee: RICH MARble. So too must the third line: an EARL'S HEIR. I do not see how the fourth line can be read with four stresses—unless one can believe either that Milton pronounced "besides" with three syllables, or that he pronounced it with two syllables but stressed the first one: BE-sides. On the linguistic evidence I am aware of, I cannot bring myself to believe either of these alternatives. The fifth line can be read as iambic, but only with something of an effort. It requires stressing "to," which does not sit well—sits even less well, indeed, in a poem marked by exactly the kind of metrical irregularities which would fit perfectly with *not* stressing "to"!

In his "L'Allegro" and "Il Penseroso," both early poems, Milton uses an alternation—to no fixed pattern that I have been able to discover—of three-, four-, and five-beat lines. (A line with three metrical feet is said to be a "trimeter" line. Two feet? "Dimeter," of course.) And the rhyming is, again, irregular to no set pattern. "At a Solemn Music" varies from three-beat to a final six-beat line. The glorious early elegy, "Lycidas," runs from three beats per line to six—and includes lines like "Through the dear might of him that walked the waves." If any seventeenth-century poet can be thought to have written a free-verse line, Milton is that poet and this is that sort of line. The conventional (agreed-upon) reading, here, is of course: THROUGH the dear MIGHT of HIM that WALKED the WAVES. But it is difficult, almost impossible, really to subordinate "dear" to "might," and I strongly suspect that Milton read the words, as I read them, as a spondee. THROUGH the DEAR MIGHT of HIM that WALKED the WAVES. This would make hash of the iambic pattern—and I think it does just that. I think, in short, that Gerard Manley Hopkins was right about Milton's heterodox (unorthodox, heretical) metrical views. With minimal resort to history, too, we can see the background which would have encouraged John Milton, classicist and devout Christian, to signal as much *dis*harmony, with the music of his verse, as he consciously tried to communicate harmony, to "justify the ways of God to man." It was Milton's England that saw the Puritan Revolution (in which he played an active and dangerous part), the revolutionary reign of Cromwell, the first and only beheading of an English king, and the vicious political and social restoration of 1660—which neither could nor in fact did endure. It was, in short, a wild, tradition destructive time. Q.E.D.

Alexander Pope is a prosodic master: no poet I know exhibits a finer, more subtle ear. But Pope's time saw a sharp (and temporary) swing to order and regularity. His metrical practice is a joy to analyze—but it is not an analysis which will much further the main outlines of this brief chapter. So, with real reluctance, I will move from Milton directly to the nineteenth century.

Nothing can shake the basic predominance of the iambic metric, in English. Pick up a geology text, or an income tax directive, or a letter from your brother, and read it with attention to stressed and unstressed syllables—that is, read it metrically. You are going to find, inevitably, that whether what you're reading is perfect iambic meter or not, it certainly and insistently tends toward iambic meter. (I have been doing this in front of classes for years. It never fails. Nor can it.) But iambic pentameter lost its stranglehold on English prosody, as the eighteenth-century esthetic faded and the heroic couplet toppled from its throne. William Blake wrote in all sorts of metrical patterns, from the very beginning. Even in "Tiriel," written in 1789 (the same year as *Songs of Innocence,* and five years before *Songs of Experience*), the partial collapse of traditional metrics is sounded:

"True, Hela, this is the desert of all those cruel ones.
Is Tiriel cruel? look! his daughter & his youngest
                                        daughter
Laughs at affection, glories in rebellion, scoffs at Love.
I have not eaten these two days; lead me to Har &
                                        Heva's tent . . ."

Jerusalem, a late poem, is far more irregular:

Into the Furnaces & into the valleys of the Anvils
                                        of Death
And into the mountains of the Anvils & of the heavy
                                        Hammers . . .

The more conservative-minded William Wordsworth, who began with poems in the heroic couplet form (as of course the very young Blake did, too), who wrote his great long poem, *The Prelude*, in blank verse, and who wrote many sonnets, also experimented in many of his shorter poems with a wide variety of prosodic patterns. Wordsworth was not a metrical innovator, but in "The Reverie of Poor Susan" he wrote in a basically anapestic line. (The anapestic metric, which later nineteenth-century poets often used, is built on a pattern of two unstressed syllables, followed by a stressed syllable. The exact opposite of the anapest, the dactyl, starts with a stressed syllable and is followed by two unstressed syllables; it is not either very natural or very common in English.)

> At the corner of Wood Street, when daylight appears,
> Hangs a Thrush that sings loud, it has sung for three
> years:
> Poor Susan has passed by the spot, and has heard
> In the silence of morning the song of the Bird.

Only the third line of this quatrain is not regular anapestic verse. In the third line, Wordsworth begins with—of course!—an iambic foot: poor SUSAN has PASSED . . . . And in his "Written in Germany, on one of the coldest days of the century," Wordsworth moves from iambic to anapestic, and back, and sometimes ends up with a line that cannot be scanned (read metrically: the process is often known as "scansion") in either of the two patterns. Here is the first of the poem's seven five-line stanzas:

> A plague on your languages, German and Norse!
> Let me have the song of the kettle;
> And the tongs and the poker, instead of that horse
> That gallops away with such fury and force
> On this dreary dull plate of black metal.

The convention would like to see that fifth line read as anapestic trimeter: on this DREAR-y dull PLATE of black MET-al. But can "black" really be subordinated, here, to "metal"? I rather doubt it. To my ear the line reads: on this DREAR-y dull PLATE of BLACK MET-al. And I am strengthened in this feeling by Wordsworth's own insistence on "the language really spoken by men," and by his observation that "there neither is, nor can be, any *essential* difference between the language of prose and metrical composition." And in a letter written in January, 1804, he further explains:

As to my own system of metre it is very simple: first and second syllables long or short indifferently *except where the passion of the sense cries out for one in preference*. Third, fifth, seventh, ninth, short etc., according to the regular laws of the iambic. This is the general rule. *But I can scarcely say that I admit any limits to the dislocation of the verse, that is I know none that may not be justified by some passion or other*. [Italics added]

When a relatively conservative poet, at least metrically speaking, can so casually dispense with what were once hard-and-fast rules, the tenure of traditional metrics is plainly threatened.

And the rest of the century demonstrates this threat in action. Tennyson's first volume, *Poems, Chiefly Lyrical*, contains poems like "Nothing Will Die," in which the content is not terribly exciting, but the metric shows a sudden break into four consecutive lines of spondees:

> Never, oh! never, nothing will die;
> The stream flows,
> The wind blows,
> The cloud fleets,
> The heart beats,
>   Nothing will die.

This same metrical variant appears also in the poem "All Things Will Die." "Leonine Elegiacs" is Tennyson's attempt to bring Greek metrics into English—not very successfully, but for our purposes, here, the failure is less important than the attempt:

> Low-flowing breezes are roaming the broad valley
>   dimmed in the gloaming:
> Thoro' the black-stemmed pines only the far river
>   shines.
> Creeping thro' blossomy rushes and bowers of rose
>   blowing bushes,
> Down by the poplar tall rivulets babble and fall.

Much of Tennyson's "The Poet's Mind" vacillates between trochaic and iambic; so too does "The Deserted House," in which the irregularities are extensive:

> Close the door, the shutters close,
>   Or thro' the windows we shall see
>   The nakedness and vacancy
> Of the dark deserted house.

The fourth line, here, is sharply irregular. Even the place-
ment of the caesura after the word "dark" makes for an
effect strangely at variance with the regularity of lines two
and three.

Browning was I think a much better poet than Tennyson,
but even in his own time it was recognized that his ear
was "rugged," different, even harsh. "The Lost Leader"—
almost certainly inspired by, if not directly an attack on,
Wordsworth—begins, for example, in a clearly tetrameter
pattern. Its meter is iambic, though many lines start with
a stressed syllable. And then comes line nine:

> We that had loved him so, followed him, honoured
> him . . .

There are four stresses, here, yes—but there are also twelve
syllables, where a four-footed iambic line would have only
eight syllables. The line seems to me a blending of a number of possible meters—and is best labelled, I think, simply
irregular, very irregular. Browning's delightful "Sibrandus
Schafnaburgensis," a lovely assault on pedantry, is written
in a distinctly irregular iambic tetrameter—and in stanza
seven suddenly breaks into a line that I defy anyone to
read as any kind of tetrameter at all:

> When the water-beetle with great blind deaf face . . .

And all these hints of metrical violence bear fruit in a poem
published in 1864, "Caliban Upon Setebos; or, Natural
Theology in the Island":

> Will sprawl, now that the heat of day is best,
> Flat on his belly in the pit's much mire,
> With elbows wide, fists clenched to prop his chin,
> And, while he kicks both feet in the cool slush . . .

Let me take this line by line. Line one can be taken as
slightly eccentric iambic pentameter: the combination of
the long vowel in "sprawl," held so long as almost to be
bisyllabic, and the caesura immediately following it, can
be understood to mark off the stress on "sprawl" from the
stress on the next word, "now." Like this: will SPRAW-ahl
NOW that the HEAT of DAY is BEST. This is surely eccentric
iambic, but the family resemblance is there. Line two can
only be taken as iambic, or indeed as pentameter, if "in"
is stressed. This is not natural, in English, but it is rather
common in Browning's metrical practice (and this is, in
itself, a clear sign of the weakening of the metrical convention, a sign that its validity has been stretched to a

tenuous thinness, that the poet can cheerfully accept artificiality of convention in order to quietly go on with his
irregular work). Even then, "much mire" is as plainly a
spondee, to my ear, as anything I have ever seen. Line
three, again, *can* be read as iambic pentameter, like this:
with ELbows WIDE, fists CLENCHED to PROP his CHIN. I
prefer to point out that trying to subordinate "fists" to
"clenched," here, for the sake of the metrical convention,
violates the much more basic rule defended so fiercely in
Wagner's *Die Meistersinger,* namely that spirit and not letter must prevail. And can even a letter-perfect reader
mangle *this* line, which comes later in the poem, into iambic pentameter:

> Loving not, hating not, just choosing so.

Read thus artificially, the line would emerge as: LOVING
NOT, HATing NOT, just CHOOsing SO. This is silly stuff—and
note that it is still not iambic pentameter. The line makes
far better sense as tetrameter: LOVing not, HATing not, just
CHOOsing SO. And what do we do with *this* later line:

> Wherefore he mainly dances on dark nights.

It reads as five stresses, surely, but "dark nights" is a
spondee, not an iamb. Or take this line, again from farther
on in the same poem:

> A tree's head snaps—and there, there, there, there,
> there . . .

The artificial, letter-perfect rule may say that this is still
iambic pentameter, like this: a TREE's head SNAPS—and
THERE, there, THERE, there, THERE. But this is certainly
nonsense—unmistakable nonsense, considered in relation
to Browning's usual rhythms, and doubly nonsense, considered in relation to this poem's rhythms. If metrical
scansion means anything, if it bears even the slightest relationship to the actual sounds of the language, this artificial reading cannot be possible. The line must be read
—and if Browning really thought differently, he was I'm
afraid wrong, but I don't think he did, or that he was—
with seven full stresses, each "there" receiving full value
as both a stress and, complete in itself, a metrical foot.
Like this: a TREE's head SNAPS—and THERE, THERE, THERE,
THERE, THERE . . . Or, for that matter, why twist "head"
into a subordinated position? Why not read the line with
eight stresses, like this: a TREE's HEAD SNAPS—and THERE,
THERE, THERE, THERE, THERE . . .

These growing metrical freedoms come to completest expression, in the nineteenth century, in the rhythmically aberrant poems of Gerard Manley Hopkins. (Significantly, Hopkins not only published little, in his lifetime, but his friend and literary executor, the poet Robert Bridges, did not feel that he could put Hopkins' work into book form until 1918, and only then after carefully preparing the way by slipping a poem here, and a poem there, into anthologies. As Poet Laureate, 1913–1930, Bridges was in a position to manage these things. And the accuracy of his judgment is indicated by the fact that, after this first collected edition appeared in 1918, no reprint was necessary for another ten years.) Hopkins' sonnet, "The Windhover: To Christ Our Lord," begins:

> I caught this morning morning's minion, king-
> dom of daylight's dauphin, dapple-dawn-drawn
> > Falcon, in his riding
> Of the rolling level underneath him steady air,
> > and striding
> High there, how he rung upon the rein of a
> > wimpling wing
> In his ecstasy! then off, off forth on swing

This can only be read by stresses, not by conventional feet. The second line, for example, has fifteen syllables, the third line sixteen, the fourth fourteen: conventional iambic pentameter has clearly been abandoned, here. And yet this is a sonnet, and it follows the Italian form, it rhymes— and it does have five stresses to a line. In an unpublished preface for an unpublished collection of his poetry, Hopkins defined this verse as "sprung rhythm":

> Sprung Rhythm, as used in this book, is
> measured by feet of from one to four
> syllables, regularly, and for particular effects
> any number of weak or slack syllables may
> be used. It has one stress . . .

In slightly over-simplified form, the scansion Hopkins would recommend for the first four lines quoted above, would look like this:

> i CAUGHT this MORNing MORNing's MINion, KING-
> > dom of DAYlight's DAUphin, dapple DAWN-drawn
> > > FALCON, in his RIDing
> of the ROLLing level UNDerNEATH him steady AIR,
> > > and STRIDing

HIGH there, how he RUNG upon the REIN of a WIMP-
ling WING . . .

I have here followed the suggestions of Hopkins' editor,
W. H. Gardner, in applying Hopkins' theory to his practice
as a poet. I would myself want to stress "LEVEL," and I
would not stress the first syllable of "underneath." I recog-
nize that, to keep five stresses in a line, one should not
stress both "steady" and "air," but I find it extremely
difficult, in reading this poem aloud, to subordinate
"steady." In any case, the basic principle is much simpler
than the elaborations which Hopkins (and sometimes his
critics and interpreters) have woven onto it. The stress,
and no longer the foot, is everything; weak, or unstressed,
syllables, no longer matter.

Hopkins tried to argue that this meant a return to the
ancient practice of the *Beowulf*-poet, in which, also, stress
was everything, and unstressed syllables did not matter
and could be accumulated or omitted, at will. He was
wrong. I do not want to discuss Old English prosody; it is
not terribly relevant—though neither is it wholly irrelevant—for modern English ears. What Hopkins *was* doing,
as I think this chapter demonstrates, was finishing off a
long and slow development in English metrics: the evolu-
tion from an omnipotent iambic metric, and especially of
an iambic pentameter metric, into a much freer era, in
which both iambic generally, and iambic pentameter in
particular, still have a place, but no longer have anything
like a monopoly—an era in which no metrical pattern has
a monopoly, even the pattern of "free (or nonconventional,
non-agreed-upon) verse." Modern poetry would have developed this freedom, had Hopkins never written a line,
or Bridges never published what he did write. The whole
six-hundred-year history of modern English prosody shows
this plainly. But Hopkins was, for all that, a great innovator, a man who not only sensed the vast movements of
history but was able to step outside of his own time and,
in a very real sense, express the future.

Which brings us to, and leaves us in, the twentieth century. Poets have, today, the freedom to rhyme or not to
rhyme, to scan or (an absurd phrase) not to scan—that is,
more accurately and sensibly, they have the freedom to use
conventional metrics if they want to, or to ignore them if
they want to. This is not however an easy freedom: it is
harder to write a good free verse poem than a good tra-

ditional sonnet or song. The traditional forms and meters sustain a poet, and limit him; they provide him with a framework in which he knows how to operate, in which the boundaries and the opportunities are basically known in advance. There is challenge in working these forms, especially in our own rather formless times, but there is also solace and comfort in their very formality. The free verse poem, on the other hand, depends a very great deal more on the individual talent of the individual poet—and each new poem is a much newer occasion for him, a much riskier and infinitely more unknown occasion, than a new poem is likely to be for traditional poets.

I do not think, myself (and T. S. Eliot has said much the same thing), that there really is any such thing as "free verse." Free from tradition, from convention—yes. But not free, surely, in the sense of having no boundaries, working under no restrictions. Poetry is, after all, musically organized language: the very fact of some organization, the necessity for some organization, means that the poet is never free. If he does not give his poem some musicality, some shape, it does not exist as a poem—and he is no poet.

TITLES OF POEMS AND PLAYS QUOTED FROM, BY AUTHOR
(Consult the Index for fuller references)

Anonymous: "Brief Autumnal"

Anwar: "In Vain"

Arnold: "Austerity of Poetry"; "Dover Beach"; "Kaiser Dead"; "Urania"

Auden: "Song for the New Year (Danse Macabre)"

Blake: "Holy Thursday"; *Jerusalem;* "On Another's Sorrow"; "A Poison Tree"; "The Tyger"; "Tiriel"

Brecht: "Against Seduction"

Browning: "Caliban Upon Setebos"; "The Lost Leader"; "Sibrandus Schafnaburgensis"; "Soliloquy of the Spanish Cloister"

Byron: "Ballad, To the Tune of 'Sally in Our Alley' "; *Don Juan;* "English Bards and Scotch Reviewers"; "I would to heaven . . ."

Carroll: "Jabberwock"

Channing: "A Poet's Hope"

Chaucer: *Canterbury Tales; Troilus and Criseyde*

Coleridge: "The Rime of the Ancient Mariner"

Corso: "Marriage"

Creeley: "The Flower"; "Like They Say"

Cummings: "Song (thy fingers make early flowers)"

Davies: "Sonnet (so shoots a star)"

Dickinson: "The Spider holds a Silver Ball"

Donne: "A Hymn to God the Father"; "A Lame Beggar"; "Song (go and catch)"; "The Sun Rising"

Drummond: "Madrigal 4"

Dryden: *Absalom and Achitophel;* "Theodore and Honoria"

Dugan: "Thesis, Antithesis, and Nostalgia"

Eliot: "The Hollow Men"; "A Song for Simeon"

Enright: "The Interpreters"

Ferlinghetti: "Autobiography"

Fitzgerald: *Rubáiyát of Omar Khayyám*

Hardy: "After a Romantic Day"

Herbert: "Jordan"; "A True Hymn"

Herrick: "On Joan"; "Upon Julia's Clothes"

Ho Chi Minh: "Prison Poem"

Hopkins: "The Windhover"

Johnson: "London"

Jonson: "Epitaph on Elizabeth, L.H."; "On my first Son"; "To the Alchemists"; "To the Reader"

Keats: "Bright star, would I were steadfast as thou art"; *Endymion;* "The Eve of St. Agnes"; "Isabella"; "La Belle Dame Sans Merci"; "On First Looking Into Chapman's Homer"; "Song (I had a dove)"; "Sonnet (when I have fears)"; "To a Cat"

Kees: "Land's End"

Lamantia: "There are Many Pathways to the Garden"

Lowell: "For Eugene McCarthy"; "Violence"

Markham: "The Man with the Hoe"

Marlowe: *Hero and Leander*

Marvell: "The Garden"; "To His Coy Mistress"

Meredith: "Song"

Milton: "An Epitaph on the Marchioness of Winchester"; "At a Solemn Music"; "Lycidas"; "On the Morning of Christ's Nativity"; "On the University Carrier . . ."; *Paradise Lost;* Sonnet 9; Sonnet 23

Morgenstern: "The Fence"

Morris: *The Earthly Paradise*

Pope: "Couplets on Wit"; *The Dunciad;* "Epigram, Engraved on the Collar of a Dog . . ."; "Epistle to Dr. Arbuthnot"; "Epitaph, Intended for Sir Isaac Newton"; "An Essay on Criticism"; "An Essay on Man"; "On a Lady who Pissed . . ."; "The Rape of the Lock"

Pound: "In a Station of the Metro"; "The New Cake of Soap"; "Salvationists: I"; "Sestina: Altaforte"

Raffel: "Interfaith Dialogue"; "Sheep-Song"

Robinson: "For Calderon"

Rossetti, C.: "Song (when I am dead)"

Rossetti, D. G.: "My Sister's Sleep"

Sappho: "If you are squeamish"

Scott: "Crocus Air"

Shakespeare: *Hamlet; King Henry the Fifth; King Lear; Loves Labours Lost; Measure for Measure; A Midsummer's Night's Dream; Othello; Romeo and Juliet;* Sonnet 73; *The Tempest; Venus and Adonis*

Shelley: *Prometheus Unbound*

Skelton: "Colin Clout"

Smart: "Hymns for the Amusement of Children . . . XXXIII"

Spenser: *Amoretti,* 30

Swinburne: "A Song in Time of Order"; "Sonnet for a Picture"

Tennyson: "All Things Will Die"; "The Deserted House"; "In Memoriam"; "Leonine Elegiacs"; "Literary Squabbles"; "Nothing Will Die"; "The Poet's Mind"

Tran Nhan-Tong: "On a Visit to Thai-Tang's Mausoleum"

Tran Te Xuong: "Graduation"

Wevill: "Caspar Hauser"

Whitman: "Song of Myself"; "To the Leaven'd Soil they Trod"; "When Lilacs Last . . ."

Williams: "It is a Living Coral"

Wolfe: *Look Homeward Angel*

Wordsworth: "It is not to be thought of"; "Lines composed a few miles above Tintern Abbey . . ."; "Lines Written in Early Spring"; *The Prelude (The Poem to Coleridge);* "The Reverie of Poor Susan"; "A Whirl-Blast from behind the Hill"; "Written in Germany"

Wyatt: "And wilt thou leave me thus"; "They flee from me"

Yeats: "Spilt Milk"; "Vacillation"

INDEX

INDEX

Names (of poets and of others), titles (of poems and of other works), significant terms and concepts, are included. A semi-colon separates primary from secondary references. No distinction is made between poems quoted in full and in part.

149

MENTOR Poetry Titles of Special Interest

☐ **ONE HUNDRED AMERICAN POEMS edited by Selden Rodman.** Selections from the colonial times to the present, including such poets as Taylor, Freneau, Emerson, Poe, Melville, Longfellow, Crane, Gertrude Stein, Jeffers, Eliot, Roethke, Lowell, and others. Introduction.
(#MT743—75¢)

☐ **ONE HUNDRED MODERN POEMS edited by Selden Rodman.** A collection designed to familiarize the reader with the main currents in American, English, and European poetry. Poets represented include Kafka, Yeats, Eliot, Sitwell, Thomas, Hopkins, Williams, Auden, MacLeish, and others. Introduction.
(#MY1071—$1.25)

☐ **THE MENTOR BOOK OF MAJOR AMERICAN POETS edited by Oscar Williams and Edwin Honig.** Selections from the work of Taylor, Emerson, Longfellow, Poe, Whitman, Dickinson, Robinson, S. Crane, Frost, Lindsay, Stevens, Williams, Pound, Moore, Ransom, Millay, MacLeish, Cummings, H. Crane, and Auden. Introduction, Notes, Index. (#MW956—$1.50)

☐ **THE MENTOR BOOKS OF MAJOR BRITISH POETS edited by Oscar Williams.** Includes Blake, Wordsworth, Coleridge, Byron, Shelley, Keats, Tennyson, Browning, Bronte, Arnold, Rossetti, Hardy, Hopkins, Davidson, Housman, Yeats, Lawrence, Muir, Owen, Graves, Barker, Thomas. Introduction. (#MW1018—$1.50)

SIGNET Classic Shakespeare

THE NEW AMERICAN LIBRARY, INC.,
P.O. Box 999, Bergenfield, New Jersey 07621

Please send me the SIGNET CLASSICS BOOKS I have checked above.
I am enclosing $_____(check or money order—no currency
or C.O.D.'s). Please include the list price plus 15¢ a copy to cover
mailing costs.

Name_____

Address_____

City_____State_____Zip Code_____
Allow at least 3 weeks for delivery